Trauma and Resilience

TRAUMA AND RESILIENCE

Your Questions Answered

Keith A. Young

Q&A Health Guides

An Imprint of ABC-CLIO, LLC
Santa Barbara, California • Denver, Colorado

Library of Congress Cataloging-in-Publication Data

Names: Young, Keith A., author.
Title: Trauma and resilience : your questions answered / Keith A. Young.
Description: Santa Barbara, California : Greenwood, [2021] | Series: Q&A
    health guides | Includes bibliographical references and index.
Identifiers: LCCN 2020027753 (print) | LCCN 2020027754 (ebook) | ISBN
    9781440870965 (hardcover ; alk. paper) | ISBN 9781440870972 (ebook)
Subjects: LCSH: Psychic trauma. | Psychic trauma—Treatment. | Traumatic
    neuroses. | Resilience (Personality trait)
Classification: LCC RC552.T7 Y68 2021 (print) | LCC RC552.T7 (ebook) |
    DDC 616.85/21—dc23
LC record available at https://lccn.loc.gov/2020027753
LC ebook record available at https://lccn.loc.gov/2020027754

ISBN: 978-1-4408-7096-5 (print)
        978-1-4408-7097-2 (ebook)

25 24 23 22 21   1 2 3 4 5

This book is also available as an eBook.

Greenwood
An Imprint of ABC-CLIO, LLC

ABC-CLIO, LLC
147 Castilian Drive
Santa Barbara, California 93117
www.abc-clio.com

This book is printed on acid-free paper ∞

Manufactured in the United States of America

Contents

Series Foreword

All of us have questions about our health. Is this normal? Should I be doing something differently? Whom should I talk to about my concerns? And our modern world is full of answers. Thanks to the Internet, there's a wealth of information at our fingertips, from forums where people can share their personal experiences to Wikipedia articles to the full text of medical studies. But finding the right information can be an intimidating and difficult task—some sources are written at too high a level, others have been oversimplified, while still others are heavily biased or simply inaccurate.

Q&A Health Guides address the needs of readers who want accurate, concise answers to their health questions, authored by reputable and objective experts, and written in clear and easy-to-understand language. This series focuses on the topics that matter most to young adult readers, including various aspects of physical and emotional well-being as well as other components of a healthy lifestyle. These guides will also serve as a valuable tool for parents, school counselors, and others who may need to answer teens' health questions.

All books in the series follow the same format to make finding information quick and easy. Each volume begins with an essay on health literacy and why it is so important when it comes to gathering and evaluating health information. Next, the top five myths and misconceptions that surround the topic are dispelled. The heart of each guide is a collection of questions and answers, organized thematically. A selection of five case studies provides real-world examples to illuminate key concepts. Rounding out each volume are a directory of resources, glossary, and index.

It is our hope that the books in this series will not only provide valuable information but will also help guide readers toward a lifetime of healthy decision making.

Acknowledgments

Many thanks to everyone at ABC-CLIO, especially Maxine Taylor, who offered this opportunity with a warm welcome and constant availability for support. Thank you also to Christine Selby, PhD, CEDS, who was kind enough to introduce me to the idea of this project and help make it possible.

I would like to acknowledge the giants in the field who have spearheaded the modern revolution in the treatment of trauma and who have guided and inspired me greatly over the years. They include Francine Shapiro, Philip Manfield, David Grand, Edna Foa, Marsha Linehan, Bessel van der Kolk, Stephen Porges, Peter Levine, Dan J. Siegel, J. Eric Gentry, Rick Hanson, Richard Schwartz, Anthony Mannarino, Judith Cohen, and Esther Deblinger.

As always, I hold heartfelt gratitude for my colleagues and supervisors, who have taught me so much over the years and continue to do so. Everything I know and do as a professional has been informed by your example and enriched by the insights you've shared.

A special thank you to two dear friends: Jim Lapierre, LCSW, CCS, who encouraged me from beginning to end in getting this book done; and James Grindle, PMH-NP, who helped ensure that my section on medication treatment for trauma is as accurate as it is. A thank you as well to Jay Graves, DC; my conversations with you helped round out my understanding of neurofeedback and how it works.

Many thanks and much love to my wife and daughters, my mother, my grandmother, my brothers and sister, my in-laws, my higher power, and all of my friends.

This book is offered with dedication to the countless survivors who inspired its development. Working with you all has helped me grow exponentially as a therapist, and I'm continually humbled and honored by your willingness to share the journey. This work is also dedicated to the survivors who are still looking for that initial foothold and a viable sense of direction—those who feel stuck, silent, invisible, trapped, or alone. I hope this book assures you that change is possible on every one of those fronts, and assists you in finding your way to the healing and recovery that you deserve.

Introduction

"So, who has heard of prolonged exposure therapy?" There was a large crowd of us, seated classroom-style at several long tables in a hotel conference room in Manchester, New Hampshire. The speaker was Dr. Edna Foa, and we'd come to learn her psychotherapy approach for post-traumatic stress disorder (PTSD). "Prior to receiving the brochure we mailed you," she said, "how many of you had heard of this treatment?" About a third of us raised our hands. "Hmm. Okay. And how many of you have heard of EMDR?" Almost the entire group put their hands in the air. She sighed and laughed to her assistant. "Ahh . . . look at that. We need to do a better job disseminating this information."

Edna Foa, PhD, would later be named one of the "Most Influential People in the World" in the May 2010 issue of *Time* magazine (Kluger, 2010). She had successfully developed one of the first and most effective modern treatments for trauma. Foa and her team were traveling the country, teaching therapists the theory behind her approach and providing a working knowledge of the skills they'd need to apply it. I was excited to be there, as a new counselor, but had no idea what "prolonged exposure" therapy was. I sat with my coworker Jude, a seasoned clinician who'd told me about the training and convinced me to come with her. Dr. Foa was one of her professional heroes.

As the morning went on, I was amazed by what I was learning. Here was a 12-week treatment that diminished symptoms of PTSD, often to a slight fraction of what they once were, for most people who completed it. The protocol is very intense. It works very quickly and incredibly well. It's also not for everybody. We watched demonstration videos of survivors talking through their trauma experiences repeatedly and in vivid detail. We saw their moments of "abreaction," as emotions they'd held for years finally found their cathartic release. My first thought, as I watched, was that this kind of approach was probably too intense for the clients I had on my caseload at that time. My second thought was that I was probably underestimating what they were capable of.

When it was time to break for lunch, I gathered my sandwich and chips from the event's assembly line and looked for Jude in the crowd. I smiled when I spotted her. Despite the fact that there were about 80 therapists in attendance, she'd somehow managed to secure two seats right next to Edna. When I sat down and joined the conversation, Dr. Foa turned to me and asked what I'd thought of the training so far. "Oh," I said, "I don't know what I was expecting, really. But, to be honest, it wasn't this. This looks very stressful to me. I mean, trauma causes so much suffering as it is. I thought you'd be showing us strategies to relax. How to find peace of mind, maybe help people forget about what happened to them so they can move on from it. You're doing the exact opposite. You're having them dive right in, and then keep diving in again and again."

"That's one of the most common misconceptions about trauma," she replied. "When we avoid reminders, try not to think about it, don't talk about it . . . that's how trauma works, and it's also what keeps the symptoms of PTSD going. You're right when you say that relaxation is necessary. You first need to know how to decrease your anxiety and feel safe. Very important. But it's not until you finally choose to stop running, and find a way to face and process what you've been running from, that the symptoms of PTSD start to weaken and you find yourself becoming stronger."

Sometimes we need to do things that feel very counterintuitive in order to get well. That can include leaving our "comfort zones" when we realize they've been holding us back. We have to learn how to quiet our inner commotion, directly challenge what trauma caused us to believe about ourselves, and introduce feelings of safety where they've been absent. When we find the courage necessary to walk safely through the monsters that chase us in our minds, those monsters that terrified us for so long, we ultimately prove that we're far stronger than they could ever be. Our steps can be large or they can be small. Either way, they carry us forward.

That lunch conversation with Dr. Foa was about 20 years ago. It was one of the initial lessons I'd learned about trauma recovery. I went on to become trained in several other treatment modalities and learned that while they do share common elements, they also work very differently. Some are fast and intensive. Others are more gradual and slowly paced. There are approaches like Dr. Foa's that involve the creation of a trauma narrative, while others employ an alternative but equally efficient means of healing. There are many well-established treatments that differ greatly in theory, even contradicting each other at times, but they've all proven their worth in helping a countless number of survivors achieve recovery and relief.

The experience of trauma is widespread. It holds a strong presence in our communities and families. Many of us know firsthand what it's like to be traumatized or the sense of helplessness we feel when we're witnessing the effects of trauma on people we care about. The goal of this book is to answer many of the questions most commonly asked by survivors and their loved ones. Most of them have to do with typical responses to trauma, why they happen, and what we can do to recover and become well. Equally important, the book answers questions about resilience. It explains how we develop a cumulative fortitude within ourselves to speed our recovery and protect us in our reactions to future adversity. My hope is also to spread awareness of the diverse and very effective therapies that are available, as well as the means to find them in your area (see the directory of resources). Trauma is a very sensitive subject that is not commonly talked about. As prevalent as it is, it's easy to feel very alone in finding the answers to many of our most important questions. I hope you find your answers in these pages and that they give you guidance in supporting the recovery of others in your life or in forging a path to it yourself.

Guide to Health Literacy

On her 13th birthday, Samantha was diagnosed with type 2 diabetes. She consulted her mom and her aunt, both of whom also have type 2 diabetes, and decided to go with their strategy of managing diabetes by taking insulin. As a result of participating in an after-school program at her middle school that focused on health literacy, she learned that she can help manage the level of glucose in her bloodstream by counting her carbohydrate intake, following a diabetic diet, and exercising regularly. But, what exactly should she do? How does she keep track of her carbohydrate intake? What is a diabetic diet? How long should she exercise and what type of exercise should she do? Samantha is a visual learner, so she turned to her favorite source of media, YouTube, to answer these questions. She found videos from individuals around the world sharing their experiences and tips, doctors (or at least people who have "Dr." in their YouTube channel names), government agencies such as the National Institutes of Health, and even video clips from cat lovers who have cats with diabetes. With guidance from the librarian and the health and science teachers at her school, she assessed the credibility of the information in these videos and even compared their suggestions to some of the print resources that she was able to find at her school library. Now, she knows exactly how to count her carbohydrate level, how to prepare and follow a diabetic diet, and how much (and what) exercise is needed daily. She intends to share her findings with her mom and her aunt, and now she wants to create a chart that summarizes what she has learned that she can share with her doctor.

Samantha's experience is not unique. She represents a shift in our society; an individual no longer views himself or herself as a passive recipient of medical care but as an active mediator of his or her own health. However, in this era when any individual can post his or her opinions and experiences with a particular health condition online with just a few clicks or publish a memoir, it is vital that people know how to assess the credibility of health information. Gone are the days when "publishing" health information required intense vetting. The health information landscape is highly saturated, and people have innumerable sources where they can find information about practically any health topic. The sources (whether print, online, or a person) that an individual consults for health information are crucial because the accuracy and trustworthiness of the information can potentially affect his or her overall health. The ability to find, select, assess, and use health information constitutes a type of literacy—health literacy—that everyone must possess.

THE DEFINITION AND PHASES OF HEALTH LITERACY

One of the most popular definitions for health literacy comes from Ratzan and Parker (2000), who describe health literacy as "the degree to which individuals have the capacity to obtain, process, and understand basic health information and services needed to make appropriate health decisions." Recent research has extrapolated health literacy into health literacy bits, further shedding light on the multiple phases and literacy practices that are embedded within the multifaceted concept of health literacy. Although this research has focused primarily on online health information seeking, these health literacy bits are needed to successfully navigate both print and online sources. There are six phases of health information seeking: (1) Information Need Identification and Question Formulation, (2) Information Search, (3) Information Comprehension, (4) Information Assessment, (5) Information Management, and (6) Information Use.

The first phase is the *information need identification and question formulation phase*. In this phase, one needs to be able to develop and refine a range of questions to frame one's search and understand relevant health terms. In the second phase, *information search*, one has to possess appropriate searching skills, such as using proper keywords and correct spelling in search terms, especially when using search engines and databases. It is also crucial to understand how search engines work (i.e., how search results are derived, what the order of the search results means, how to use the snippets that are provided in the search results list to select websites, and how to determine which listings are ads on a search engine results page). One also has to limit reliance on surface characteristics, such as the design of a website or a book (a website or book that appears to have a lot of information or looks aesthetically pleasant does not necessarily mean it has good information) and language used (a website or book that utilizes jargon, the keywords that one used to conduct the search, or the word "information" does not necessarily indicate it will have good information). The next phase is *information comprehension*, whereby one needs to have the ability to read, comprehend, and recall the information (including textual, numerical, and visual content) one has located from the books and/or online resources.

To assess the credibility of health information (*information assessment* phase), one needs to be able to evaluate information for accuracy, evaluate how current the information is (e.g., when a website was last updated or when a book was published), and evaluate the creators of the source—for example, examine site sponsors or type of sites (.com, .gov, .edu, or .org) or the author of a book (practicing doctor, a celebrity doctor, a patient of a specific disease, etc.) to determine the believability of the person/ organization providing the information. Such credibility perceptions tend to become generalized, so they must be frequently reexamined (e.g., the belief that a specific news agency always has credible health information needs continuous vetting). One also needs to evaluate the credibility of the medium (e.g., television, Internet, radio, social media, and book) and evaluate—not just accept without questioning—others' claims regarding the validity of a site, book, or other specific source of information. At this stage, one has to "make sense of information gathered from diverse sources by identifying misconceptions, main and supporting ideas, con-flicting information, point of view, and biases" (American Association of School Librarians [AASL], 2009, p. 13) and conclude which sources/ information are valid and accurate by using conscious strategies rather than simply using intuitive judgments or "rules of thumb." This phase is the most challenging segment of health information seeking and serves as a determinant of success (or lack thereof) in the information-seeking process. The following section on Sources of Health Information further explains this phase.

The fifth phase is *information management*, whereby one has to orga-nize information that has been gathered in some manner to ensure easy retrieval and use in the future. The last phase is *information use*, in which one will synthesize information found across various resources, draw conclusions, and locate the answer to his or her original question and/or the content that fulfills the information need. This phase also often involves implementation, such as using the information to solve a health problem; make health-related decisions; identify and engage in behaviors that will help a person to avoid health risks; share the health information found with family members and friends who may benefit from it; and advocate more broadly for personal, family, or community health.

THE IMPORTANCE OF HEALTH LITERACY

The conception of health has moved from a passive view (someone is either well or ill) to one that is more active and process based (someone is working toward preventing or managing disease). Hence, the dominant focus has shifted from doctors and treatments to patients and prevention, resulting in the need to strengthen our ability and confidence (as patients and consumers of health care) to look for, assess, understand, manage, share, adapt, and use health-related information. An individual's health literacy level has been found to predict his or her health status better than age, race, educational attainment, employment status, and income level (National Network of Libraries of Medicine, 2013). Greater health literacy also enables individuals to better communicate with health care providers such as doctors, nutritionists, and therapists, as they can pose more relevant, informed, and useful questions to health care providers. Another added advantage of greater health literacy is better information-seeking skills, not only for health but also in other domains, such as completing assignments for school.

SOURCES OF HEALTH INFORMATION: THE GOOD, THE BAD, AND THE IN-BETWEEN

For generations, doctors, nurses, nutritionists, health coaches, and other health professionals have been the trusted sources of health information. Additionally, researchers have found that young adults, when they have health-related questions, typically turn to a family member who has had firsthand experience with a health condition because of their family member's close proximity and because of their past experience with, and trust in, this individual. Expertise should be a core consideration when consulting a person, website, or book for health information. The credentials and background of the person or author and conflicting interests of the author (and his or her organization) must be checked and validated to ensure the likely credibility of the health information they are conveying. While books often have implied credibility because of the peer-review process involved, self-publishing has challenged this credibility, so qualifications of book authors should also be verified. When it comes to health information, currency of the source must also be examined. When examining health information/studies presented, pay attention to the exhaustiveness of research methods utilized to offer recommendations or conclusions. Small and nondiverse sample size is often—but not always—an indication of reduced credibility. Studies that confuse correlation with causation is another potential issue to watch for. Information seekers must also pay attention to the sponsors of the research studies. For example, if a study is sponsored by manufacturers of drug Y and the study recommends that drug Y is the best treatment to manage or cure a disease, this may indicate a lack of objectivity on the part of the researchers.

The Internet is rapidly becoming one of the main sources of health information. Online forums, news agencies, personal blogs, social media sites, pharmacy sites, and celebrity "doctors" are all offering medical and health information targeted to various types of people in regard to all types of diseases and symptoms. There are professional journalists, citizen journalists, hoaxers, and people paid to write fake health news on various sites that may appear to have a legitimate domain name and may even have authors who claim to have professional credentials, such as an MD. All these sites *may* offer useful information or information that appears to be useful and relevant; however, much of the information may be debatable and may fall into gray areas that require readers to discern credibility, reliability, and biases.

While broad recognition and acceptance of certain media, institutions, and people often serve as the most popular determining factors to assess credibility of health information among young people, keep in mind that there are legitimate Internet sites, databases, and books that publish health information and serve as sources of health information for doctors, other health sites, and members of the public. For example, MedlinePlus (https://medlineplus.gov) has trusted sources on over 975 diseases and conditions and presents the information in easy-to-understand language.

The chart here presents factors to consider when assessing credibility of health information. However, keep in mind that these factors function only as a guide and require continuous updating to keep abreast with the changes in the landscape of health information, information sources, and technologies.

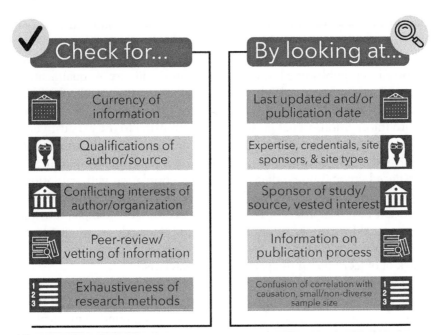

All images from flaticon.com

The chart can serve as a guide; however, approaching a librarian about how one can go about assessing the credibility of both print and online health information is far more effective than using generic checklist-type tools. While librarians are not health experts, they can apply and teach patrons strategies to determine the credibility of health information.

With the prevalence of fake sites and fake resources that appear to be legitimate, it is important to use the following health information assessment tips to verify health information that one has obtained (St. Jean et al., 2015, p. 151):

- **Don't assume you are right**: Even when you feel very sure about an answer, keep in mind that the answer may not be correct, and it is important to conduct (further) searches to validate the information.
- **Don't assume you are wrong**: You may actually have correct information, even if the information you encounter does not match—that is, you may be right and the resources that you have found may contain false information.
- **Take an open approach**: Maintain a critical stance by not including your preexisting beliefs as keywords (or letting them influence your choice of keywords) in a search, as this may influence what it is possible to find out.

- **Verify, verify, and verify**: Information found, especially on the Internet, needs to be validated, no matter how the information appears on the site (i.e., regardless of the appearance of the site or the quantity of information that is included).

Health literacy comes with experience navigating health information. Professional sources of health information, such as doctors, health care providers, and health databases, are still the best, but one also has the power to search for health information and then verify it by consulting with these trusted sources and by using the health information assessment tips and guide shared previously.

Mega Subramaniam, PhD
Associate Professor, College of Information Studies,
University of Maryland

REFERENCES AND FURTHER READING

American Association of School Librarians (AASL). (2009). *Standards for the 21st-century learner in action.* Chicago, IL: American Association of School Librarians.

Hilligoss, B., & Rieh, S.-Y. (2008). Developing a unifying framework of credibility assessment: Construct, heuristics, and interaction in context. *Information Processing & Management, 44*(4), 1467–1484.

Kuhlthau, C. C. (1988). Developing a model of the library search process: Cognitive and affective aspects. *Reference Quarterly, 28*(2), 232–242.

National Network of Libraries of Medicine (NNLM). (2013). Health literacy. Bethesda, MD: National Network of Libraries of Medicine. Retrieved from nnlm.gov/outreach/consumer/hlthlit.html

Ratzan, S. C., & Parker, R. M. (2000). Introduction. In C. R. Selden, M. Zorn, S. C. Ratzan, & R. M. Parker (Eds.), *National Library of Medicine current bibliographies in medicine: Health literacy.* NLM Pub. No. CBM 2000-1. Bethesda, MD: National Institutes of Health, U.S. Department of Health and Human Services.

St. Jean, B., Taylor, N. G., Kodama, C., & Subramaniam, M. (February 2017). Assessing the health information source perceptions of tweens using card-sorting exercises. *Journal of Information Science.* Retrieved from http://journals.sagepub.com/doi/abs/10.1177/0165551516687728

St. Jean, B., Subramaniam, M., Taylor, N. G., Follman, R., Kodama, C., & Casciotti, D. (2015). The influence of positive hypothesis testing on youths' online health-related information seeking. *New Library World*, 116(3/4), 136–154.

Subramaniam, M., St. Jean, B., Taylor, N. G., Kodama, C., Follman, R., & Casciotti, D. (2015). Bit by bit: Using design-based research to improve the health literacy of adolescents. *JMIR Research Protocols*, 4(2), paper e62. Retrieved from http://www.ncbi.nlm.nih.gov/pmc/articles/PMC4464334/

Valenza, J. (2016, November 26). Truth, truthiness, and triangulation: A news literacy toolkit for a "post-truth" world [Web log]. Retrieved from http://blogs.slj.com/neverendingsearch/2016/11/26/truth-truthiness-triangulation-and-the-librarian-way-a-news-literacy-toolkit-for-a-post-truth-world/

Common Misconceptions about Trauma and Resilience

1. ANYONE EXPOSED TO A TRAUMATIC EVENT WILL DEVELOP PTSD

Trauma doesn't affect everyone the same way, and living through a horrible life experience doesn't necessary mean that we'll develop PTSD because of it. In situations where multiple people are exposed together to the same traumatic event, they can respond individually in very different ways. Take, for example, the scenario of a public bus, full of passengers, that gets into a major accident. Some of those passengers may become terribly traumatized almost immediately and have enduring symptoms from that point forward. Others may believe they handled the accident pretty well, only to have symptoms of PTSD manifest days or weeks afterward. And there could be others who never develop PTSD from the experience. They may show some initial signs of post-traumatic symptoms that last briefly and then alleviate on their own or even get through the ordeal without any significant stress reaction at all. However, members of this third group may have completely different outcomes if they encounter other traumas later in life. Surviving an adverse event and emerging relatively unscathed doesn't necessarily mean we won't develop PTSD if another trauma occurs. Our responses fall upon a spectrum of vulnerability and resilience, and there are many factors that play into both sides. The more resilience we have, the more fortified we are when these events take place. See questions 1, 8, 9, 21, 22, and 23 for more information about the varied impacts of trauma, and the internal defenses that can be discovered and strengthened within us.

2. PEOPLE WITH PTSD CANNOT RECOVER

Recovery from PTSD is possible. Remarkable discoveries and advancements have been made in the fields of neuroscience and mental health treatment, particularly over the last 30 years. They've given us a much broader understanding of what trauma is, the effects of trauma on the brain, and the kinds of treatments and coping skills that work the most effectively in alleviating trauma. Recovery from PTSD can be generally defined as (1) relief from trauma-related symptoms and (2) the resolution of the problems they cause in our lives. Beyond that, it's defined and achieved uniquely according to each survivor's personal beliefs, goals, and priorities. Each person's path to success in trauma recovery is a combination to be unlocked, and there are many treatment approaches and ideas that can help. While some of them differ greatly in how they work, we've learned an awful lot about characteristics that most successful paths to recovery have in common. As long as a survivor persists and continues to step forward, gaining insight from the journey and applying it to the approach, the potential for advancement toward recovery continues to exist. Turn to questions 26, 29, 45, and 46 to read more about recovery and the means to achieve it.

3. YOUR LEVEL OF RESILIENCE IS BEYOND YOUR CONTROL; YOU EITHER HAVE IT OR YOU DON'T

The term "resilience" refers to our resistance and adaptability to adverse and stressful events. While there are factors in early childhood development that can grant us an advantage of resilience from the beginning, it can be depleted over time, at any age, by the challenges we face and how they affect us. There are also measures we can take to improve it. It's never too late to establish a foundation or to build upon what we have. We achieve this by tending to our emotional injuries, improving our self-care, training new habits of wellness into our life choices, and connecting in healthy relationships with others. Survivors of trauma generally show lower levels of resilience when they have active symptoms of

PTSD. Fortunately, the same treatments that help facilitate recovery tend to bring a lasting boost in resilience as well. Please refer to questions 21 through 25 and questions 30 through 40 to learn more about how this is accomplished.

4. PEOPLE NEED TO FULLY REMEMBER THE DETAILS OF THEIR TRAUMA IN ORDER TO ACHIEVE RECOVERY

When we've experienced something shocking and traumatic, those memories aren't typically stored the same way as memories in everyday life. If the brain is too distressed to properly register and integrate what has happened, it holds the unprocessed memory in raw and emotionally charged fragments. Sometimes it resorts to a very sophisticated defense mechanism where it "blocks" material of these fragments from our conscious recollection. This is an automatic safeguard, the brain's instinctive effort to prevent overload and maintain some level of equilibrium. The blocked material may be a few missing minutes or details of what happened or large spans of time left inaccessible in our minds. This can be very frustrating, and survivors who have blocked memories will often surmise that they can't adequately recover unless they can somehow gain access to them. Conversely, people who have full custody of every detail of what happened often feel that it's more of a curse than a blessing and believe that progress would be much easier if they could only bring themselves to forget. Neither situation categorically prevents us from succeeding in recovery. We don't need to remember comprehensive details to heal from the effects of trauma, and if we've been haunted by full and vivid memories for years, we have access to that same capability and potential. Questions 9, 26, 28, and 29 provide more detail about the recovery process and how memories and reminders of trauma are involved in it.

5. THERE IS A COMMON TREATMENT THAT HELPS EVERYONE

There are specialized treatments validated for trauma, which have shown consistently impressive outcomes in research and in practice. Evidence-based therapy modalities like eye movement desensitization and reprocessing, prolonged exposure therapy, and trauma-focused cognitive behavioral therapy have excellent success rates and often decrease symptoms to the point that people no longer meet criteria for a diagnosis of PTSD. But there's no such thing as a treatment that works 100 percent of the time or one that proves to help everyone to the same extent. There are many explanations for this. Some therapies may be too intensive and stressful for some survivors at certain points in their recovery process. Even when they're able to engage fully with treatment, it's still possible that they won't see the desired results from any particular approach regardless of its overall rate of success. Some people find great benefit from medications commonly prescribed for trauma symptoms. Others experience little to no relief from them or get unpleasant side effects more than anything else. There are survivors who thrive by connecting with others in processing support groups, and others who show more progress in individual therapy. The pursuit of "what works best" is a learning process. The good news is that if one treatment idea doesn't succeed, it doesn't mean that the others won't. It's also possible that a method found to be unproductive in early stages of recovery may be more effective when it's applied later. Sometimes we need to work on building more of a foundation of stabilization and safety before we'll succeed in climbing beyond it. Persistence, patience, and adaptability are ultimately the keys to success. The path forward clarifies with every step taken and every lesson learned. Questions 26 and 29 explore characteristics commonly shared between modern treatment approaches for trauma, and questions 30 through 40 cover some of the unique differences that set them apart.

QUESTIONS AND ANSWERS

The Basics

1. What is trauma?

This first question is by far one of the most important because our efforts
to recover from trauma become more informed when we start from an
accurate understanding of what it is and how it works. Trauma is an experience or series of experiences that is perceived as so distressing, threatening, or shocking that it overwhelms the mind's capacity to effectively
process and contain it. It can come from an isolated event or result more
progressively from a buildup of physiological stress that accumulates over
time. Arguably defined as more of an injury than an illness (Zimbardo,
Sword, & Sword, 2012), the effects of trauma can be found in our brains,
minds, bodies, and relationships. We can achieve healing and recovery
across these same four dimensions. While the symptoms of PTSD can be
as confusing as they are debilitating, they're signs of a natural and predictable reaction from a healthy brain and its effort to ensure our survival
after a traumatic event.

Generally speaking, our brains are remarkably well equipped to manage the normal stresses of daily life. When we encounter common situations that cause us discomfort (like hearing a disturbing story on the
news or realizing we're going to be late for work) we can usually cope
with them pretty easily and without much effort. We quickly deal with
the burden of the moment, put it into perspective, and establish its place

proportionately in our memory of what happened that day. These routine stressors come and go, and they don't tend to bother us for very long.

When we're faced with something unusually upsetting but not beyond the horizon of what we can handle (like the end of a serious relationship or the loss of a job), we then have a deeper level of processing to do. We'll need to think it through more thoroughly and turn to our loved ones for support. As human beings, we're social animals, so we take refuge in our relationships. We connect with others. We talk, express the emotions that we feel, possibly have a good cry, and derive some personal insights and lessons where they can be found. We synthesize the meaning of our painful experiences until we feel ready to move on.

However, when an event is so distressing and unacceptable that we reach a point of overwhelm, and it breaches the threshold of what we can tolerate, the inner brain will intervene and react automatically with its own defensive measures. This is true regardless of whether we're children or adults. It's true whether the trauma lasts 30 seconds or is something we're forced to endure for years on end. When the brain is overburdened by what it's facing, it won't prioritize the need to process what's happened, or connect with others, or figure out how the situation fits within the grand scheme of our lives. It sacrifices these efforts in favor of directing all of its energy into simply surviving the experience. It quickens our heartbeats, energizes our bodies, and heightens our perception of what we need to worry about most. This is our psychological "survival mode," a necessary and functional activation meant to keep us alive through times of crisis.

Ideally, once the danger has passed, these mechanisms relax, recalibrating us from a state of overwhelm back to a feeling of safety. As it does, we find it easier to reflect on what we've been through. We learn from it. We talk it out, feel what we need to, and plan ways to move forward. We're able to work through the crisis that once overwhelmed us and resign it to the past, much as we would do with lesser stressors.

But when our brains' protective measures don't alleviate with time, when they sustain that state of reactive overwhelm and continue to prioritize survival indefinitely, recovering from the event becomes much more difficult. Unprocessed stress is accumulated and stored within the mind and body, producing the natural signs and symptoms of a post-traumatic response. In essence, the activation of our instinctive survival mode gets stuck in the "on" position, afflicting us with the weight of that storage until it's effectively accessed and properly worked through.

To get a more comprehensive understanding of what trauma is, we can define it from the angle of each dimension it affects.

The impact of trauma on the brain can be understood by the initial shock reflex that it elicits and how that response is maintained thereafter. We react to shocking and threatening events in the moment with an automatic surge of energy that is directed into what are commonly referred to as "fight," "flight," and "freeze" responses. The experience of having PTSD is arguably an extended and recurrent manifestation of this energy. The autonomic nervous system involved in this process has two branches: the sympathetic, which is what energizes us to respond to stress, and the parasympathetic, which helps with digestion, regulating heartbeat, and rest. When the sympathetic branch is disproportionately and continuously activated (a state known as "sympathetic dominance"), we remain in a physiological state of anxious arousal. This brings lasting shifts in neurotransmitters, like serotonin and dopamine, which modulate our mood and stress responses, and norepinephrine, which calls our minds to alert and sharpens our awareness. Stress hormones like adrenaline and cortisol are released, sometimes continually and long after the traumatic event has passed. The body registers these changes and keeps itself energized, aroused continually by a sense of threat (Sherin & Nemeroff, 2011). This translates to disturbances in concentration and sleep. We find ourselves more easily irritated. It becomes harder to derive enjoyment from our hobbies and interests. On a cellular level, the brain establishes and reinforces neural pathways with a bias toward fear and shame, shifting our beliefs about ourselves, raising suspicions of others, and shaking our sense of safety in the world around us. The areas of the brain responsible for detecting and interpreting when we're at risk, including the amygdala and hippocampus, play key roles in sustaining these changes. They're activated by trauma into a state of constant vigilance and assumption of danger (Morey, Haswell, Hooper, & De Bellis, 2016).

These reactive changes in the brain are mirrored by subjective shifts in the mind. The neurological bias that locks us into an assumption of continued threat also makes us feel regularly compelled to escape it. Our minds interpret this as a crucial need to avoid anything even remotely reminiscent of the trauma, even if we're aware that our methods are irrational. We might no longer feel safe wearing the same outfit or riding in the same car as we did that day. Situations that make us feel vulnerable or exposed can feel unbearable, so we reduce our interaction with others and retreat into simple, isolative routines. We may no longer tolerate people standing behind us, going to parties, walking through crowds, or sleeping with the lights off. Thoughts and memories come to feel like threats in themselves.

Conversation about our experiences with trauma can feel difficult or next to impossible. Interpreting and expressing our emotions require that we feel safe enough to explore them, and our capacity for introspection becomes stifled when we're overcome by anxiety. This compromises our ability to work through what happened and find meaning from having survived it, which, in turn, inhibits us from recovering. Trauma leaves an untold story stuck within our minds, scattered in fragments of emotionally charged memories without an integrative narrative to hold them together. Working through that story feels counterintuitive and dangerous because any attempt to put the pieces together risks reactivating the brain's fear-based avoidance response. On the other hand, if we follow that avoidance instinct and try not to think about it at all, we find ourselves constantly thwarted by invasive memories, nightmares, flashbacks, and trigger responses. The same brain that continually sounds the alarm and issues the warning not to think about our traumas also doesn't seem keen on letting us move on from them. This renders our emotions compressed and trapped. Until our experiences are adequately processed and integrated, our minds will be stuck in a state of perpetual reaction to them and will be prone to waves of anxiety, anger, guilt, and helplessness.

The echoes of that untold story are contained physically as much as mentally. We feel the somatic sensations of long-held emotional wounds. We can feel them in the pits of our stomachs. They emanate in our throats, in our hearts, and across our necks and shoulders. These feelings can register in sensation from head to toe, and our bodies will guard instinctively against them with tension of muscles and a protective collapse in posture, much like it would with a physical injury. The body shares the burden of our traumas until our emotions are given proper release.

Our conscious connection to these physical sensations may also be compromised. Rather than inciting an increased sensitivity to where our emotions are held in the body, our brains may cope instead by distancing them from our awareness. Our mind-experience dissociates from our body-experience, causing us to feel numb to the sensations that our emotions create. This is an involuntary defense mechanism. It makes it harder to tend to the emotional suffering that our bodies hold and to access and understand the important messages contained within. Meanwhile, whether we're numbed to these sensations or not, this somatic distress is often accompanied by the continuous release of stress hormones. This increases our body's vulnerability to systemic inflammation and can render us more susceptible to certain medical conditions later in life (see question 10).

The impact of psychological trauma is also found and very much felt in our relationships with others. Symptoms of PTSD affect our ability to trust, to relate, to communicate, and to experience relational feelings that would otherwise be readily accessible. We may find ourselves internally detached from feelings of love and happiness, even when we're wholeheartedly devoted to connection in our relationships. This could be because we've become dissociated from our emotional awareness, a result of our brains avoiding pleasant feelings as much as any other. It can also be a result of feeling too much: the fear, shame, or irritability shining so brightly that we can't let our guard down enough to notice other emotions behind them. This makes it very difficult when we're trying to explain the complexity of our symptoms to our loved ones. When our brains and bodies are actively inhibiting us from accessing and understanding what we feel inside, it only makes sense that we'd also struggle with articulating it to others.

These are some of the more typical long-term effects of severe trauma. They're the signs of survival mode mechanisms that have been stuck in a state of activation, which are mitigated and alleviated as we progress in recovery. It bears repeating that living through a traumatic event doesn't necessarily mean that we'll have profound or lasting problems from it. And regardless of whether we've been affected by trauma or not, there are protective attributes we can strengthen within ourselves that will fortify us against stressful and negative experiences in the future. They collectively play an integral role in how effectively we cope with adversity when it happens and in how quickly we're able to recover when it's depleted us. These qualities constitute our resilience, and they can be found and developed across the same dimensions of our lives where trauma affects us the most.

2. What are the different trauma conditions, and how are they diagnosed?

There are several trauma conditions diagnosed in the field of mental health. They have some aspects in common but are distinguished from each other according to the amount of time that has elapsed since the traumatic event, the age of the person being diagnosed, the nature of the impact from the symptoms, and the severity and duration of them. Formal diagnoses are commonly defined by the criteria outlined in the *Diagnostic and Statistical Manual of Mental Disorders*, which at the time of this printing is in its fifth edition. It's often referred to as the *DSM–5* (American Psychiatric Association, 2013).

Mental health professionals who are trained and qualified to diagnose trauma conditions include psychiatrists, psychologists, physicians, psychiatric nurse practitioners, counselors, and social workers. A diagnostic evaluation is achieved through clinical interview. There are also psychological tests that can be used to evaluate trauma symptoms through a standardized series of questions. A trauma condition can only be diagnosed if the symptoms aren't likely to have been caused by medical issues or the use of substances. This is because some medical conditions or effects of alcohol or drugs can sometimes mimic symptoms characteristic of a trauma response and need to be ruled out for a psychiatric diagnosis to be viable.

The most commonly referenced and recognizable trauma condition is post-traumatic stress disorder (PTSD). PTSD can be diagnosed in both adults and children. The criteria that justify a diagnosis of PTSD include identification of the traumatic event or events and sufficient symptomatic evidence of having been traumatized. These criteria are conventionally categorized among

1. Intrusive symptoms (e.g., memories of trauma repeatedly pushing their way into our minds, nightmares directly or symbolically related to what happened, flashback experiences);
2. Active efforts to avoid the topic of what happened (in thought and conversation) and/or efforts to stay away from external cues (people, places, things, or situations) that remind us of what happened but would otherwise be considered safe;
3. Changes in our mood and thinking in reaction to the trauma; and
4. Signs of autonomic arousal from having been traumatized (e.g., our minds and bodies feeling "charged up" by internal alarms, feeling continually activated by an uncontrolled sense of fear, an ongoing sense of vigilance and assumption of danger in our daily lives).

A diagnostic formulation for an adult relies primarily upon the survivor's report of symptoms, while the effects of trauma on a child are often observed more behaviorally by caretakers and service providers. A diagnosis of PTSD means that these symptoms have had a significant impact on the person's ability to function in life and have been present for more than a month. If these symptoms are present but it hasn't yet been a month since the traumatic event, the diagnosis used for that period of time is called "acute stress disorder."

PTSD can be diagnostically specified as "complex" when the trauma is not the result of an isolated, time-limited event or of a relatively finite set of events but rather a drawn-out and long-term exposure to one or more traumatic circumstances, relationships, or environments. Examples could be a pattern of sexual, emotional, or physical abuse of a child; institutional traumatization (like living in an abusive or dangerous group home, school, cult, or prison); or surviving a long-term abusive relationship as an adult. Complex trauma can have a deeply rooted impact on a person's sense of identity and worldview. This brings some additional factors to consider in the recovery process, with regard to pacing treatment productively, securing a sense of safety, and establishing a healthy support system.

Attachment disorders are conditions that originate in early childhood, typically when children are exposed to abuse or neglect, don't have consistent caregivers (e.g., children moving from foster home to foster home) or access to their caregivers, or are otherwise adversely affected through their interaction with people responsible for their care. Unlike adults, who can exercise more independence when it's safe to do so, young children don't have the choice to fight or to flee a dangerous or neglectful home. They can only adapt to the situation they're stuck in and resort to building relationships with the adults available to them (often the sources of abuse or neglect) for the sake of survival. For that reason, children will learn to interact in abusive or neglectful homes in a way that ensures that their needs are at least partially met. They learn to become keenly aware and reactive to signs of anger and mood shifts in adults and develop unique coping strategies to live around these dangers. These survival responses become interwoven within the development of a child's capacity for tolerating distress and within the child's understanding of how social interaction works. While attachment disorders are diagnosed when children are young (when symptoms are present before the age of five), the beliefs children establish about themselves and about the world tend to persist as they get older. Until these disorders are resolved, they often translate to difficulty establishing a sense of self, feeling safe in the world, trusting others, and forming and keeping relationships.

There are two attachment disorder conditions in the *DSM–5*. The first is reactive attachment disorder. Otherwise known as an "avoidant" attachment response, children with reactive attachment disorder will cope with distress by withdrawing into themselves and will ignore or reject efforts from adults who try to comfort them or connect with them socially. The second is disinhibited social engagement disorder. This attachment response expresses in an opposite direction in that children will approach and trust adults indiscriminately, with little to no understanding of boundaries or the sort of caution that should be maintained with strangers. Both of these conditions develop when children haven't yet learned how to form secure child-to-adult relationships.

The developmental complications that manifest into attachment disorders can also be associated with personality disorders later in life (Levy, Johnson, Clouthier, Scala, & Temes, 2015), especially when other vulnerability factors are in place. Personality disorders are deeply rooted patterns of thinking and behavior that become evident during adolescence or early adulthood. They have a serious negative impact in relationships and in overall life functioning. While other personality disorders may have developmentally traumatic origins, borderline personality disorder is one that often stands out in research and discussion about trauma, owing to its frequent association with neglectful, invalidating, and abusive childhood experiences (see question 14).

Adjustment disorders are diagnosed when a life change or stressful event causes an unusual and lasting amount of distress. The symptoms can come in the form of anxiety, depressed mood, or changes in behavior that may be considered disproportionate in reaction to what happened. Adjustment disorders are only diagnosed, however, when these symptoms wouldn't be better explained by a different diagnosis (like depressive disorders, acute stress disorder, PTSD, or other anxiety disorders).

Trauma-related diagnoses can also include what's called an "other trauma- and stressor-related disorder" and an "unspecified trauma- and stressor-related disorder." These diagnoses are used when trauma-related symptoms have inflicted a substantial impact on a person's well-being or ability to function but haven't met enough criteria to justify any of the other stress- or trauma-related diagnoses. The difference between them is that other trauma- and stressor-related disorder includes an explanation in the diagnostic narrative as to why those criteria haven't been met, and a diagnosis of unspecified trauma- and stressor-related disorder doesn't come with that description. An adequate explanation may not be possible at the time of an assessment. A diagnostician might see evidence of a traumatic response but may not yet have enough detail to clarify what exactly is happening and why. Psychiatric diagnoses exist to provide direction for treatment, and formulating the most accurate impression can be a work in progress. Diagnoses can and should be corrected and updated as more information is learned and the clinical picture clarifies over time.

3. How common is trauma in the United States?

If we define the term "trauma" more broadly, it would be fair to say that we've all experienced it. It's impossible to completely avoid suffering through life, and that suffering sometimes comes in large doses. It would be reasonably expected, for example, for someone to experience some kind of serious medical illness, the end of a relationship, or the loss of a loved one in the course of his or her life. By and large, the fallout of these typical events may not approach the level of a diagnosable disorder. But it's also possible that what might be considered a comparatively minor normal life event for some may be a source of oppressive and lasting distress for others. Parents getting divorced may be a relatively smooth transition for one child but a world-shaking disaster for the child's brother or sister. A car accident may be brushed off relatively easily by the driver but severely traumatizing for the passenger. The effects of trauma are unique to each individual, and people will react differently to different kinds of events. The degree of severity depends in large part on how much the event psychologically damages and follows a person over time.

Because of this variety and spectrum of impact, when considering the prevalence of trauma in our society, we can't simply look at rates of PTSD diagnoses and call them the entire picture. Traumatized people who don't meet full criteria for a diagnosis are still legitimately traumatized and can benefit from the same strategies and treatment options that are validated for that purpose. We must also consider that there are many people who would absolutely meet full criteria for PTSD (and sometimes have no idea that they would) but haven't been given the formal diagnosis, either because they haven't engaged in mental health treatment or because their symptoms and trauma history haven't been adequately understood or addressed by health-care providers.

If we look at rates of trauma in the United States, we can consider the numbers as they differentiate between young children, older children, and adults. According to a 2010 report by the National Child Traumatic Stress Network, one study showed that a little more than half (52.5%) of surveyed children ages two to five have experienced a traumatic stressor in their lifetime. Research the National Center for PTSD (NCPTSD) references on its website states that 15–43 percent of girls and 14–43 percent of boys have gone through at least one trauma, and of those children who have, 3–15 percent of the girls and 1–6 percent of the boys develop PTSD (2019a). According to the NCPTSD, about six out of every 10 men and five out of every 10 women will experience at least one significant trauma in their lives, and about eight million people have PTSD in a given year (National Center for PTSD, 2019b). A systemic review of collective research has shown that 5–10 percent of the general population will develop full PTSD in the course of their lifetimes (Greene, Neria, & Gross, 2016).

Despite its considerable presence in families, neighborhoods, schools, colleges, workplaces, and our military, the true prevalence of trauma still isn't widely known or acknowledged in our culture. Because of this, survivors often live under the impression that they're alone in what's happened to them, feel confused and alienated by their symptoms, and worry that they won't be understood by others. The truth is that there are many among us who can relate very much to how they're feeling and what they're going through. Our communities benefit from every effort we make to increase awareness and education about the prevalence of trauma and its effects as well as the professional treatments for trauma that are widely available.

4. What types of events and experiences are the most likely to cause trauma?

It's important to acknowledge that any attempt to list some of the most common causes of trauma will risk giving the impression that any one of these sources of suffering (or those not mentioned) qualifies more or should be more highly prioritized than others as traumatic events. There are countless scenarios in which we can be hurt by accidents or trage-dies, and a vast variety of ways that we can be damaged by other human beings. It would be impossible to list them all, and attempting to com-pare the legitimacy of trauma between the stories of any two survivors would be an unfair and fruitless exercise. For this reason, the examples offered in answer to this question are presented in no particular order, and without any insinuated comparison of the severity of damage that they cause. Suffice it to say that if you've jumped to this question to validate whether your experience counts as a traumatic event, the answer would be a resounding yes, to whatever degree you've been traumatized by it.

The most likely causes of trauma generally involve an assault or serious threat on a person's safety, basic dignity, or sense of worth. They leave the survivor feeling endangered, attacked, violated, deprived of basic rights or survival needs, or subjected to another person's abusive control. They are assaults and shocks to the physiological system, pushing the brain beyond its capacity to register and tolerate what's happened. When trauma histories are screened upon intake for mental health services, initial assessments include questions about history of physical assault or abuse, emotional or psychological abuse, sexual assault or abuse, and neglect. These categories represent some of the most widespread and common sources of trauma.

Physical assault or abuse can come in the form of a single event or a pattern of repeated violence. Common sources include domestic violence from partners, abuse from parents or other family, or criminal acts of violence, such as robberies, road rage confrontations, or hate crimes.

Emotional abuse means being attacked verbally, threatened, degraded, or bullied. Bullying has unfortunately evolved over time as a cause of trauma and taken some sinister new forms with the advent of the internet and social media platforms: it's become much easier to degrade someone publicly and on a much wider scale. While emotional abuse or bullying in previous generations meant being harassed either alone or in the presence of peers, more recent generations have had the added burden of photos or videos shared online, which exponentially magnifies the scope of their humiliation. Emotional abuse is sometimes differentiated and at other times used interchangeably with the term "psychological abuse," though psychological abuse is used more often to describe situations when someone has been stalked, tracked or/monitored, controlled, manipulated, "gaslighted" (encouraged to doubt the judgment or sanity of oneself), or otherwise terrorized, with or without the added impact of direct physical harm.

Sexual assault or abuse is unfortunately a very common source of trauma, and the damage it causes can be complicated by several factors. For one thing, it's much more common to be sexually assaulted by someone we know than by a stranger. According to the Rape, Abuse & Incest National Network (RAINN), 8 out of 10 rapes are committed by someone known to the survivor, with a third of them committed by relationship partners or former partners. In their online review of sexual abuse cases reported to law enforcement, it was found that 93 percent of juvenile victims knew the perpetrator ("Perpetrators . . . ," n.d.). While sexual assault of any kind is traumatizing in itself, we suffer from additional dynamics of betrayal when it comes from a relationship we once trusted. It can be confusing and complicated when we've established bonds of love with or dependence on the perpetrator, as these feelings can persist even when we've removed ourselves from the threat and acknowledged the abuse for what it was. This is particularly true when the sexual abuse comes from a parent or other relative, a trauma more commonly shared in our communities than most of us would dare to guess.

The effects of abuse can become more compounded when a survivor is captive to the danger for any prolonged period of time, whether in a situation of abuse in the household, during incarceration, through sex trafficking, or in any other residence or institution where the victim feels confined and abuse is taking place. While certainly taking nothing away from the horror of any single traumatic event, there's an additional dimension of hopelessness when the home we return to is not a safe place or an abusive environment is otherwise felt to be inescapable. When daily life brings the anticipation of being victimized, whether at predictable times of the day (e.g., an abusive alcoholic parent who only drinks in the evening) or without any means of guessing when the attack will occur (e.g., living with people who are prone to sudden, violent outbursts), it perpetuates a constant and costly state of vigilance and dread.

"Neglect" is a term most typically applied to children, the elderly, and incapacitated adults in that it involves either deprivation of basic survival needs (food, shelter, opportunity for hygiene) or emotional isolation and invalidation from those people charged with a survivor's care. While the trauma of neglect may or may not be accompanied by the added detriment of physical, emotional or psychological, or sexual abuse, the profound, complex, and lasting damage that it can cause on its own should never be underestimated. Studies have consistently shown that neglect can have devastating fallout on a survivor's development of a sense of self, personality development (Khaleque, 2015), learning capability, and ability to connect with and build relationships with others (Mayer, Lavergne, Tourigny, & Wright, 2007).

There is a multitude of other life experiences that can have a lasting and traumatic impact. These include accidents, natural disasters, a pronounced loss of freedom or identity, a shocking and disruptive change in life, experiences in military service, traumatic grief, or medical trauma. "Traumatic grief" is a term used when a grief process has been compounded by a concurrent trauma response to an overwhelming loss. This can happen from witnessing the sudden or unexpected death of a loved one, such as a parent losing a child or a child losing a parent. Medical trauma can originate from problems with severe birth complications, waking during surgery, or invasive procedures that cause extreme pain or horror. While trauma responses typically come from firsthand experience, they can sometimes be provoked by witnessing a traumatic event happening to someone else (like an accident, violence, murder, or a physical or sexual assault).

It bears repeating that a trauma response isn't necessarily attributable to a single event. Sometimes it emerges more gradually, generated by an incremental buildup of distress that wears our resolve and resilience down until we finally reach a breaking point. This is common in the professional lives of first responders like police officers, paramedics, and firefighters. It's experienced by veterans who cope with horrible things they've seen by mentally burying what happens each day for the sake of moving on to the next objective. Cumulative trauma is also common in neglect situations, abusive relationships, and other predicaments that leave survivors feeling trapped in overwhelming circumstances for prolonged periods of time.

5. Are certain groups of people more likely to experience trauma than others?

While any one of us can be affected by traumatic experiences, there are people who, because of their situations, environments, or identities, are statistically more prone to them.

One such group would be children. It's often said that children are resilient, which can be very true at times, but it would be fair to say that they're also something of an easy target. For one thing, they aren't armed with the power of choice that comes from independence and self-efficacy. They're equipped only to the degree that they are allowed to be and only according to how they're taught. Children are bestowed with all of the healthy benefits and all of the adversity that their household situation permits and don't have a say as to which environment they're born into. If supportive and healthy relationships with other adults aren't offered or available to them, they have no means of knowing the proper steps to reach out for help. And with so little life experience behind them, they don't have the basis for comparison to distinguish between what is their fault and what isn't. According to developmental psychologists, children are capable of feeling shame very early in development—sometimes as young as age two—long before they develop the maturity to independently determine what they should and should not internalize as a reasonable punishment for their own behavior (Belsky & Domitrovich, 1997). They depend upon parents and other adults for that guidance, and in the absence of it, kids will often blame themselves and take abusive situations as a measure of their own worth.

It may seem redundant to identify people exposed to domestic violence as notably vulnerable to trauma, but they're also too prominent a group to be excluded, especially when you consider how remarkably common abusive relationships are in our society. The National Coalition Against Domestic Violence (NCADV, n.d.) has reported that one out of four women and one in nine men have experienced severe domestic violence. These numbers aren't entirely inclusive because they don't acknowledge the children who are living as witnesses to abuse of a parent or are subjected to the abuse themselves. The National Child Traumatic Stress Network found that anywhere between three million and 10 million children are exposed to domestic violence in the United States every year (NCTSN, n.d.). In a national telephone survey it conducted in 2017, the NCTSN learned that one in 15 children reported witnessing violence in the home. NCTSN reasoned that these numbers were probably optimistic because it couldn't gather data to adequately represent the experiences of children ages six years and younger (NCTSN, 2018).

The first population that comes to mind for many people who hear the term "post-traumatic stress disorder" is our veterans and active duty military. This association has strong historical underpinnings because our diagnostic understanding of trauma and its categorization of symptoms originated from observation of its impact on soldiers (Anders, 2015). Our military personnel deal with unimaginable horrors of combat, including regular threat of death, exposure to extreme violence, and the shock of surprise gunfire and explosions. They sustain injuries and witness violence not only toward their fellow soldiers but also against the enemy they're fighting and the collateral damage inflicted upon civilians. In one study of more than 88,000 service members who were returning from deployment to Iraq, up to 70 percent of soldiers reported at least one combat exposure while in service overseas (Simiola & Norman, n.d.).

Difficulty with reintegration into civilian culture can exacerbate problems for many military personnel, including those who never saw combat. In his article titled "How PTSD Became a Problem Far beyond the Battlefield," published in *Vanity Fair* (Junger, 2015), as well as his online TED talk (Junger, n.d.) on the same subject, award-winning journalist and war reporter Sebastian Junger noted that while only 10 percent of our military engage in combat, more than 50 percent of them file for benefits due to problems from PTSD. He explained that the symptoms of trauma can have much more opportunity to flourish when returning veterans no longer have the group cohesiveness that they experienced overseas and that their resilience is significantly compromised by the harsh contrast of isolation they often feel after they've returned home. This culture shock and sense of solitude may be a salient contributing factor in the alarming rate of veteran suicides in the United States, reported by the Department of Veterans Affairs (2018) to be more than 6,000 suicides each year from 2008 to 2016.

Sexual assault is another predominant cause of trauma in the military and at alarming rates. The U.S. National Center for PTSD reported that according to its data, 23 percent of women have reported sexual assault in the military, and 55 percent of women and 38 percent of men have suffered sexual harassment (PTSD, 2018). In the RAND Corporation's Military Workplace Study, it was found that approximately 1 percent of men and 4.9 percent of women experienced a sexual assault over the course of one year. These percentages translated to an estimated 10,600 servicemen and 9,600 servicewomen (Morral et al., 2015).

College students are also at high risk for sexual assault. According to RAINN, 23.1 percent of female undergraduates and 5.4 percent of male undergraduates experience rape or sexual assault through physical force or incapacitation ("Campus Sexual Violence," n.d.). When considering rates of assault in military environments, on college campuses, and elsewhere, we must remember and account for the fact that these numbers are limited only to when those assaults were reported and suitably acknowledged. While surveys and studies provide a good general idea of the scope of these problems, there will reliably also be a silent number of survivors who aren't represented in those percentages.

People living with alcohol or drug addiction are another group more prone to trauma histories or symptoms of PTSD. A question that often follows consideration of that fact is "Which came first?" Does trauma lead to addictive behavior, or does addiction lead to trauma? Research shows a correlation from both directions. Studies have found people diagnosed with PTSD to be much more likely to have a substance abuse disorder than people who haven't been traumatized, and people who seek treatment primarily for addiction show strikingly high lifetime PTSD rates, ranging from 30 percent to more than 60 percent (McCauley, Killeen, Gros, Brady, & Back, 2012). A mind in chronic distress will be desperate to seek relief, and survivors suffering from the terror of the past will often look for ways "not to feel." Someone who hasn't been traumatized prior to developing an addiction will often be subjected to dangerous situations and more susceptible to becoming traumatized by the amplifying demands of addiction and the hazards associated with active use.

People in the LGBTQ+ community are at an elevated risk for trauma. In a 2015 survey of 10,528 students between the ages of 13 and 21, across all 50 states, it was found that 85.2 percent of LGBTQ+ students were verbally harassed, 13 percent were physically attacked, and almost half of them (48.6%) experienced online harassment and cyberbullying. Almost 60 percent of those students reported being sexually harassed. This torment can bring fatal results, as LGBTQ+ youth were found to be almost five times as likely to have attempted suicide compared to heterosexual youth (Kosciw, Greytak, Giga, Villenas, & Danischewski, 2016). According to research referenced by the Trevor Project, 40 percent of transgender adults reported having made a suicide attempt in their lives, 92 percent of which occurred before the age of 25.

The homeless population at large, and particularly those who are child and teenage runaways, are statistically more endangered. There are a variety of risk factors associated with homelessness that reduce resilience and make the homeless more vulnerable to trauma, including but not limited to malnourishment, lack of family or other supports, untreated medical conditions, exposure to poor weather, and mistreatment by others. A report by the National Coalition for the Homeless stated that people experiencing homelessness are not only very often disregarded, marginalized, and dehumanized in our culture but also live in a world of increased jeopardy for violence, sexual assault, harassment, abduction, and other hate crimes (Leomporra & Hustings, 2018). In one study that covered five U.S. cities, 49 percent of respondents reported being the victim of an attack, and of those people, 72 percent of the victims reported being attacked one to three times while homeless (Meinbresse et al., 2014). Children and teens who have run away or are otherwise without a home are more vulnerable to exploitation. There is, unfortunately, a booming industry driven by predators who target youth for purposes of abduction and sex trafficking. Out of the 23,500 runaways reported to the National Center for Missing and Exploited Children in 2018, an astounding rate of one in seven were identified to be likely victims of sex trafficking.

Refugees, having been forcibly displaced from their homes, are another group of people who have higher rates of trauma. They're often fleeing countries where living conditions have become dangerous and intolerable, and they may have the added stress of family separation and a need to acclimate to a new culture and language. Refugees often live with the aggregate effects of traumatic experiences that accumulated until they were finally able to escape. Collective studies have shown a prevalence of depression and PTSD among refugees—15 percent and 30 percent, respectively—and have identified exposure to torture and the cumulative shock of multiple traumatic events to be the most reliable predictors of these high rates (Silove, Ventevogel, & Rees, 2017).

Professional first responders commonly suffer from the accrued burden of repeated traumatic events as well. Police officers, firefighters, paramedics, and other rescue workers are repeatedly subjected to scenes of accidents, violence, abuse, and death. Because of the unpredictable nature of their jobs and their daily exposure to these situations at times, they are at unusually high risk for secondary traumatic stress (trauma symptoms caused from witnessing the trauma of others). Research has shown that in addition to contending with the effects of violence and injury, first responders have an increased susceptibility to trauma because of the repeated discovery of abuse to children in the course of their work (Levy-Gigi, Richter-Levin, & Kéri, 2014). It only makes sense, then, that child welfare workers also belong on this list. While they may not fall into the category of first responders, their job by definition involves hearing the details of countless child abuse cases. A practice brief provided by the ACS NYU Children's Trauma Institute (2012) identified physical risk, exposure to child abuse and neglect, working with incomplete information, and a negative bias in public opinion about their profession to contribute to secondary traumatic stress in child welfare workers and turnover in their field. They found in surveys that 50 percent of these workers had "high" or "extremely high" risk of compassion fatigue (another term for secondary traumatic stress) and that, in a survey of child welfare professionals across five states, more than 50 percent of respondents reported feeling trapped and endangered in the course of their required work.

People who are incarcerated show a higher risk for trauma too. As mentioned in the answer to question 4, losing our freedom and feeling captive in a dangerous environment brings an added level of complexity to our trauma responses. The day-to-day routine and culture of prison life carry considerable risks, and that nearly constant need for situational awareness can be exhausting. As weeks and months pass, a tremendous amount of stress accumulates from maintaining it. Research has shown that traumatic symptoms in inmates are exacerbated by their constant state of hypervigilance in prison life and also by the need to repress stress and emotions to avoid unnecessary attention and conflict (Haney, 2001). It's quite typical in prison populations to find previous histories of trauma as well. One study found that in the United States, one in six male inmates reported being physically or sexually abused before the age of 18 and that more than half of them reported experiencing physical trauma as a child (Wolff & Shi, 2012).

This is a fitting segue to the final group that's more vulnerable than others to experiencing trauma in our society: people who have already been traumatized. Survivors living with symptoms of PTSD have an increased risk of susceptibility for being traumatized again, for a variety of reasons. A decrease in resilience from previous traumas can generally render us more vulnerable to the impact of future traumatic events. There are additional and more specific risk factors, which are explained in more detail in the answers to questions 15, 16, 18, and 19.

6. I've heard of people reacting to horrible things with a "fight, flight, or freeze" response. What is this, and what determines the response that we choose?

The term "fight, flight, or freeze" refers to the activation of an immediate trauma response when we encounter a threatening or shocking event. It's an instinctive survival mechanism orchestrated between the brain and the autonomic nervous system that propels us physiologically into a course of action without bothering to wait for our conscious minds to weigh in with an opinion. For that reason, to whatever extent this reactive process is activated in the moment, we don't get to choose ahead of time whether our brains energize us to take flight or fight our way out of a situation or freeze our bodies into a state of protective arrest. As the psychiatrist and trauma expert Bessel van der Kolk, explained eloquently in his book, *The Body Keeps the Score*, when provoked to a fight, flight, or freeze response, the brain devises a strategy on its own with a "pre-programmed escape plan," and we're left afterward to make sense of what happened (van der Kolk, 2014, p. 57).

Consider a scenario where a mother is shopping with her two children in a mall and hears gunshots. Her brain's reflex response may be to make herself small by crouching to the ground and remaining perfectly frozen like a statue, possibly pulling her children toward her as she does it. She may dissociate (see question 13), become faint, or pass out completely. On the other hand, if she's cornered and the gunman is in her line of sight, she may be galvanized to charge at him and unleash a fury that she never knew she was capable of. She may use that energy to grab her kids and duck into one of the stores as fast as they can move, hiding in the aisles or crawling through them to find an exit. Or this mother may just instinctively run and may or may not think to grab or shout to her children as she goes.

The course of action that we take can lead to confusion and distress as we reflect afterward on what happened. The mother who grabs her kids and runs for the exit might find herself coming to full cognitive control as she stands outside in the parking lot; she may wonder for a panicked moment where her children are, even if they're still in her arms. The mother who attacks the gunman may struggle to give police an accounting of the events because she propelled herself forward without planning any particular way to defend herself. The mother who leaves her children behind may run outside and reorient, only to run back into the mall for them after she's realized what's happened.

It can be easy to feel frustrated or guilty in retrospect, if our brains' initial responses weren't what we would have preferred in that moment of crisis. If that's the case, it's important to keep in mind that we're judging ourselves for a fight, flight, or freeze response that was executed before we had the neocortical functioning to choose it. The brain steps forward and tries to ensure our survival in the most heroic way it knows how, in the moment, before we get our bearings cognitively and have a chance to fully contemplate our options. We have that response mechanism to credit for whatever it decided to do in that first reactive impulse, regardless of whether it went ultimately right or wrong.

People may also react to danger by sacrificing themselves to save or protect others. This flies in the face of the theory that our brain's mechanism always prioritizes its own survival over anything else. Others might respond to crisis by engaging the person posing the threat with compassion and an effort to communicate. It's a point of consideration as to whether these are variations of the instinctive fight, flight, or freeze response, a reaction that's different but similarly automatic, or more of a conscious and intentional choice.

There is an understandable commonsense line of thinking that specific training or preparation for traumatic events (like doing safety drills, learning martial arts, or getting a gun for self-defense and learning how to shoot) or taking some level of professional training (as a paramedic, police officer, or soldier) is a means of influencing which reflex response our minds will choose in the future. This may be true, but training by itself doesn't necessarily offer any guarantees. Seasoned soldiers and police officers might still freeze up in a situation, even if they've handled a similar event effectively in the past. Accumulated trauma or stress may have depleted their resilience over time, activating a fight/flight/freeze response that they may not have experienced before.

At the same time, training and preparation can make a big difference in how we handle future situations, especially when our resilience is otherwise strengthened. As we learn new skill sets for problem solving and for crisis management, and gain practice and confidence in applying those skills, we can decrease the probability that the inner brain will startle so quickly into an automatic response when a crisis occurs. Our reactions become much more measured and deliberate when we're slower to overwhelm. Resilience in the face of crisis is bolstered by an informed awareness of what we're capable of handling and reinforced by the safety and support we feel in our relationships with others. The renowned neuroscientist Stephen Porges, PhD, found that enhancing our sense of internal safety helps inhibit the fight, flight, or freeze response from happening (Porges, 2009) and that the quality of our social connection and engagement can be a primary measure in achieving this (Porges, 2003).

The fight, flight, or freeze response is a split-second reactive function of our hard wiring; it's meant to keep us alive when we're overcome with a dangerous situation. While we don't get to choose how our brain reacts when it's shocked into that function, we can take steps to build resilience and decrease the likelihood that it will overwhelm so quickly to begin with.

7. I experienced something that most people would consider traumatic, but I don't feel traumatized. Is this normal?

There are several reasons why this might happen. The explanation with the most positive outlook would be a matter of resilience. The event may not have raised your distress beyond the threshold that would provoke a post-traumatic response. Certain adverse events that affect some people greatly may be handled and effectively processed by others, particularly when resilience factors are in place. These factors can include, among other things, how much of a sense of control and efficacy they felt at the time of a traumatic event, how adaptive and confident they were in their ability to get through it, how supported they felt by others, how much opportunity they had to process what happened afterward, and how much stress occupied their minds and bodies through this time.

Some of these resilience factors are also context-specific and depend, in part, on our understanding of the situation. Imagine, for instance, a refugee who's stopped by police in the United States for a traffic violation. If the refugee had fled a home country where law enforcement was corrupt and getting attacked or unjustly imprisoned by police was commonplace, then any perceived verbal aggression or physical contact by the police officer would have a much higher chance of creating a trauma reaction. If someone else was in the same situation, but life had taught that person that being stopped by the police was pretty safe, it would be a completely different encounter. There is the trauma event itself, and then the matter of how it's perceived and taken in through the lens of each person's world-view and life experience. If prior experience has taught you to assume that a situation's inescapable and you may be under the threat of death, the chances of becoming traumatized reasonably increase. On the other hand, if you've survived a very threatening and dangerous experience but didn't realize how threatening and dangerous it was until well after the fact, your brain may have been spared the shock that would otherwise have pushed it to become overwhelmed.

Another possibility would be that you were, in fact, affected by the event, but the feelings haven't yet emerged in a way that you can identify. People will sometimes feel more "stunned" than distressed in their initial reaction to a traumatic event. They might show all appearances of being okay but then have a delayed stress response later down the line. You may or may not notice more thoughts and feelings emerging in the future. If that happens, use your supports, talk these things through when you're ready, and do what's necessary to take good care of yourself. If you find that any problems rise to a need for professional mental health care, those services are available if you need them.

More severe problems can be delayed as well. Traumatic stress is often endured by a conscious or subconscious "survive and get through it" mentality. When we push that distress away to the corners of our minds for the sake of moving past it, the cumulative burden of that effort is maintained physiologically. First responders will sometimes cope with horrible scenes they've witnessed by "compartmentalizing" the day's work in their heads, leaving it behind them as they go home, and hoping that their brains reset by the next shift. They file it away and carry on, day by day, week by week, until the filing cabinet is full and the compartments reach a critical mass. One day there may be an unusually stressful moment that finally causes those files to spill, triggering a sudden and confusing cascade of symptoms. Unprocessed trauma doesn't tend to cooperate when we try to simply dismiss and forget about it.

Other times, ironically, an added measure of safety is what makes the difference. A sexual-assault survivor may experience more intrusive and explicit symptoms only after having received news that the perpetrator wound up in jail or died. Post-traumatic reactions can be relatively hidden from our conscious awareness for periods of time until they're "green-lit" to come forward by a brain that's either triggered to action or convinced it's finally and sufficiently out of harm's way.

It could also be that symptoms of PTSD have already presented themselves, but the emotional effects of them are distanced from the person's ability to feel them. A traumatized brain will sometimes take the route of anesthetizing itself with feelings of numbness, dissociating (see question 13), partially or fully blocking emotions or memories of the event, or distancing its awareness of sensations in the body. This would mean that you won't necessarily "feel traumatized" but only because your brain has removed that feeling from your range of perception until it decides what to do next. In this case, it would be less likely for you to believe you were entirely unscathed from the traumatic event because the unusual absence of feeling, memory, or sensation would be evidence to the contrary.

The Effects of Trauma

8. What happens to the mental health of someone who becomes traumatized?

While the effects of trauma are summarized in questions 1 and 2, there is certainly more to be said about how trauma can affect our thinking and overall mental health. If we reduced human suffering to its most raw material, if we opened our traumatized hearts and converted our emotional wounds into language, the most predictable spoken messages behind our pain would be "I'm not safe," "I'm not good enough," and/or "I'm unlovable." As core beliefs, these messages are strong and resistant to change. They fester like mental infections, inflicted from injuries of the past, and become conflated with our perspectives of ourselves, other people, and life in general. These words are burned by trauma into the lenses of our worldviews and will maintain themselves in one form or another until they've been properly processed and modified.

It should come as no surprise that a deeply rooted belief of "I'm not safe" would be a natural outcome of being traumatized. When our bodies and minds have been activated into a combined state of avoidance and fear, we feel a push to urgency by alarms going off when there's no fire. This can create difficulty in trusting others, a regular need to scan surroundings for signs of danger, or an intolerable rush of fear when someone is standing behind us or passing outside our line of sight. For sexual-assault survivors, it makes physical intimacy difficult or impossible at times and triggers panic even from safe touch or the process of routine medical exams. A lack of a sense of basic safety is like living with a blaring racket of noise running constantly in the background, a perpetual call of impending threat. This can quickly exhaust a survivor's resolve and patience through the course of the day and bring rises in irritability and anger, especially in times of increased stress.

A particularly haunting question that will often weigh heavily in the mind of the survivor is "Why me?" This is a loaded question with an inherent bias toward self-blame, inviting internal responses that very often boil down to variations of "I'm not good enough" or "I'm unlovable." This is one of the most predictable outcomes of being abused, neglected, attacked, or otherwise victimized by crime. We attack ourselves in retrospect just for being in that situation. We ridicule ourselves with what we know now but didn't know then. We scrutinize how we handled it and burden ourselves mercilessly with judgment about "what that means." Lacking anything else, we may reason that we must have done something previously in life, perpetrated some crime that adversely affected our karmic balance, to have deserved something that terrible. This happens even when we've been traumatized by accidents. Whatever form our self-blame takes, we may believe it completely or just "feel like it's true," even when we know rationally that we weren't responsible. Survivors ask questions like "What did I do to bring this on myself?" or "What could I have done differently to prevent this, and why didn't I do that?" Our self-blame compounds when more traumatic events follow. If we've survived a series of abusive relationships, our thinking will often justify our shame by mistaking a correlation for a causation: "Well, the common denominator in all the relationships is me." "It must mean I cause this somehow, or attract it, or bring it out in people." These beliefs are pilot lights for excessive and undeserved guilt, which generalizes into a habit of scapegoating ourselves whenever it flares. This can feel like an unnamed daily pressure to apologize at every possible opportunity. It can show in the form of sleepless nights, agonizing in hindsight for anything we've said or done imperfectly on any given day.

These belief patterns are incredibly strong, and because of them, it can be hard for survivors to talk to others about what they've been through. The fear and shame they so often feel is driven and kept alive by the same repetitive thoughts and beliefs that stifle their ability to communicate. "I'm not safe" translates into "Talking about it would be dangerous" or "My mind will finally break entirely if I do this." "I'm not lovable" branches into "It's my fault" and "People will either get angry with me, or they'll realize how disgusting I am if they know the truth." And the core message of "I'm not good enough" predicts that we could never be strong enough to talk about it, that we aren't worth the effort, or that we won't be believed by anyone even if we did. It can lead us to doubt our own credibility, even when we know every word of our account to be absolutely true.

Despite how convincing they feel, these harsh targeted judgments against ourselves are not truths. They're called "cognitive distortions." They come in the form of extremes because a traumatized mind will be much more likely to sustain an exaggerated negativity bias and to see things in concrete, black-and-white terms. Our conclusions float to the margins and become more binary, which in turn creates mental "rules" that are stacked against us. If we don't feel completely safe, we must be in some kind of danger. If we don't match up to our idea of perfect, it must mean we deserve to be despised. The idea of a "gray area" (e.g., that yes, things happen, but going for a walk should be reasonably safe most of the time) sounds much less realistic. When our thinking is influenced by the effects of trauma and the anxiety of sympathetic dominance (see question 1), our view of reality is more likely to be interpreted through a forced mental imperative to assume the worst in order to survive.

In his cognitive theory of depression, psychiatrist Aaron Beck developed a point of reference known as the "cognitive triad." He explained that depression commonly affects three aspects of the way we think: our view of ourselves, our view of the people and world around us, and our view of the future (Beck, Rush, Shaw, & Emery, 1987, p. 188). The mental effects of trauma can easily be translated into these same three categorizes. Trauma is unique, however, in that it can make our view of the future much harder to imagine. Having a brain in survival mode means that it's focusing on getting us through the trials and the perceived dangers of the here and now. This makes it very challenging to envision and plan for what life may look like months or years down the road. Trauma and fear suppress creativity, making it much more difficult to fantasize about long-term goals and consider future possibilities.

While cognitive distortions may be deeply rooted, they're not permanent fixtures. Worldviews can readjust, and survivors can be freed from the tyranny of what trauma has pushed them to believe. When the underlying pain is processed and steps toward recovery are achieved, the same plasticity of the neural pathways in the brain that allowed for these beliefs to set in also allows for them to be corrected. As we progress in becoming well, internal alarms quiet. Peace of mind replaces fear. This allows creativity to emerge and the "gray area" of life to come back into view. Shame alleviates, and the responsibility and blame for what happened shift and find their way to where they belong. Survivors' perception of their own value comes back into focus.

One possible exception to the examples of cognitive distortions mentioned above would be a situation of traumatic grief from the loss of a loved one. Grief can absolutely include cognitive distortions, but it's otherwise a unique journey in itself with regard to its impact on mental health. It has additional facets to it, including the meaning of the relationship and the loss, a survivor's spiritual beliefs (or lack of them), and how the grief changes shape over time. Several of the treatments that are covered in later answers (e.g., EMDR, trauma-focused CBT) that are validated specifically for trauma can be very effective in helping people through a grief process as well.

9. How can trauma affect a person's memory?

Because trauma overpowers the coping capacity of the brain, our memories about it function differently and can be much less cooperative than memories that feel safe and normal. In day-to-day life, when we recall a benign memory from a typical day, we're able to pull it to the forefront of our minds pretty easily. Parts of our recalled memories get highlighted according to the context of what we're thinking or talking about and the aspects of the story that we find relevant or personally meaningful. Every time we retrieve a memory into our present consciousness like this—that is, for the purpose of thinking and communicating about it—we run the possibility of altering it slightly and having the memory influenced and replaced in an updated form by the story we just told (Bridge & Paller, 2012). This is a normal process and just part of how our brains work. After we're done talking and the story reconsolidates back into our long-term memory, it can go back as a retouched version. The differences may be very minor, but this is why you can have several friends recalling the same vacation they took together, or the same funny story on a night out, and get some marginally different takes on what happened. They may have started off as very similar narratives but evolved differently according to the values and needs of each of the brains that stored them. Our memories are somewhat malleable in that regard and are meant to mold meaningfully as they're synthesized into our autobiographical narrative, those "stories about us" that help us understand our identities, what we believe, and how we've grown.

Traumatic memories differ greatly in how they're kept in the brain. They're often fragmented and can sometimes be stored out of chronological order, like an image or a message on a puzzle that was dropped and scattered. The memory is suspended as raw material, unprocessed and not yet integrated into a closed story of the past with a beginning, middle, and end (Bedard-Gilligan, Zoellner, & Feeny, 2017). That puzzle may come with the added frustration of having missing pieces in key locations. Our brains will sometimes block access to traumatic memories, either in bits and pieces or in large measure. Memories that we do have may have specific points of focus because when we're threatened or in the process of being traumatized, our attention will sharpen and sometimes become limited to what's threatening us. As a trauma survivor, you may struggle to recall characteristics of your attacker's face or the clothing the attacker was wearing but have no problem remembering in great detail the weapon that was pointed at you. Alternatively, our more accessible memories may have less to do with what was threatening and more to do with what wasn't.

The effects of trauma don't just affect our memories of the trauma themselves. They also have an indirect effect on forming new memories. Nightmares, anxiety, intrusive memories, and body activation from stress hormones can all play a part in disrupting sleep. When our brains don't get adequate rest, our capacity for memory suffers. Insomnia can have a substantial impact on overall cognition as well as working memory and memory consolidation. A lack of sleep further activates the sympathetic nervous system, which in turn releases more stress hormone (cortisol). This creates a pattern of sleeplessness and subsequent memory problems that compounds upon itself (Alhola & Polo-Kantola, 2007).

Several psychotherapy treatment modalities have developed from the theory that if traumatic memories are properly accessed, expressed, and processed, without inducing overwhelm, the emotional charge that they hold becomes neutralized. When they're given structure and effectively worked through, our trauma memories have a chance to reconsolidate not as broken fragments but as autobiographical events that happened and then ended, finally taking their definitive places as remnants of the past, as normal memories would. These therapy approaches employ a variety of specialized techniques to facilitate this process (see "Treatment Options & Recovery"). Unprocessed memories appear to be a driving force behind symptoms of PTSD, and safe integration of those memories into a structured trauma narrative can be a central means of resolving them.

10. Can traumatic experiences contribute to medical conditions?

The extent of the body's involvement in housing the effects of trauma cannot be understated, and this is reflected in the drastically increased rate of medical conditions experienced by trauma survivors. Traumatic experiences have been found to have substantive effects on our physical health, often originating from events in childhood and persisting across the life span.

When we're traumatized, as adults or as children, our bodies produce an overabundance of stress hormones, including cortisol and adrenaline (Pan, Kaminga, Wen, & Liu, 2018). These hormones serve an important purpose, as they energize us to get through moments of crisis and help ensure our survival when it's threatened. In ideal circumstances, once the threat has passed and we've regained an inner felt-sense of safety, they reflect this change by regulating naturally back to their baseline levels. But when a trauma response endures over time, maintaining itself physiologically and indefinitely, our production of stress hormones remains elevated. As months and years pass, the accumulated effects of a perpetual state of stress, sometimes referred to as an "allostatic load," take their toll on the body. This brings long-term consequences on the nervous, endocrine, and immune systems, throwing the body into a state of chronic inflammation (Danese & McEwen, 2012).

We learned a great deal about this subject from a groundbreaking study that was conducted from 1995 to 1997 at the Kaiser Permanente Clinic in San Diego, California. The research team gathered data in confidential surveys from more than 17,000 members of a health maintenance organization and evaluated how childhood abuse and neglect correlated with increased rates of health problems later in life. This investigation was called the CDC-Kaiser Permanente Adverse Childhood Experiences (ACE) study, referred to in short as "the ACE studies." Questions were added to an existing evaluation, asking participants about adverse (traumatic) events that occurred before the age of 18. The questions screened the patients for history of emotional abuse, physical abuse, and sexual abuse as children, as well as exposure to household violence. They also asked whether the participants grew up with addiction in the household, mentally ill relatives, or a family member who was imprisoned ("About the CDC-Kaiser ACE Study," n.d.).

The number of adverse experiences that each participant had prior to the age of 18 translated into an "ACE score" ("Got Your ACE Score?"

2018). In correlating these scores with health issues later in life, the results were shocking. The ACE studies showed us that people with a score of four or more adverse childhood experiences were more than twice as likely to have ischemic heart disease or chronic obstructive pulmonary disease (COPD) as adults. They were found to be more than two times as likely to have a stroke later in life, almost twice as likely to have cancer, and 1.6 times more likely to have diabetes (Felitti et al., 1998). Subsequent research has shown that systemic inflammation from the shock of trauma and its physiological effects create an elevated risk for chronic disease and can subsequently bring an overall reduction in life expectancy (Kelly-Irving et al., 2013).

While childhood trauma increases our vulnerability to these conditions, there are also wellness and resilience factors that play an important role in preventing or decreasing our risk. Studies have repeatedly shown that a child's established resilience can have a significant protective effect in preventing future health problems (Traub & Boynton-Jarrett, 2017). And if we've suffered trauma as children, effective mental health treatments for PTSD and other steps taken in recovery can bring relief of symptoms and make room for a corresponding increase in resilience when we're older. Even if our bodies have already been ravaged by stress hormones into adulthood, we can decrease systemic inflammation by building resilience later in life, particularly by establishing healthy social relationships (Spencer-Hwang et al., 2018).

While trauma appears to weaken our defenses and leave us more susceptible to medical conditions later in life, there are exceptions to the trend. Progress in recovery and the development of resilience can award an alleviating effect on the chronic body inflammation that would render the body more susceptible to these conditions and decrease the potential for further damage if we've already been afflicted by it.

11. How can trauma affect our relationships with others?

Trauma can have a strong impact on our relationships with supports and loved ones, and relationships can have an equally significant influence on our recovery process. Unfortunately, like many issues related to mental health, the symptoms typical of trauma aren't commonly known or talked about. When they happen to us or to someone we love, we often don't know what to expect. This presents a steep learning curve for both ourselves and our support systems. Families, partners, and friends who want desperately to be supportive often find that the specifics of how to help can feel like uncharted territory (see question 42).

A sense of distance can form in relationships when trauma symptoms are happening, and this can happen for many reasons. When we've been traumatized, we'll often hesitate to share our symptoms, even (and sometimes especially) with loved ones, in part because we feel embarrassed, fear being thought of or treated differently, or irrationally blame ourselves (see question 8). Intrusive memories and an internal sense of foreboding push us to avoid thinking or talking about what happened. Chronic anxiety and stress translate into emotional sensitivity and agitation and can make even minor relationship conflicts feel infuriating. Hypervigilance wears our resolve to the point that simply being observed by others feels uncomfortable. Irritability and eruptions of anger leave loved ones feeling attacked, or like they need to walk on eggshells, as much as it saddens us to wonder why we've become so prone to lashing out. Activities that we used to love may now fall completely out of our interest. If we've been patient and affectionate in the past, we may now seem irritable and remote. An agonizing distance can be felt in relationships that were once very close. When dissociative symptoms are happening (see question 13), they diminish our capacity to access and share our emotions and stresses. We can otherwise have difficulty expressing how we feel or recognizing emotions in ourselves or others (a condition called "alexithymia"), which brings its own host of challenges. All of these symptoms make it easy to feel very alone even when we're surrounded by supports. It's awfully hard to offer answers and explanations to someone else when we're asking ourselves the same questions.

Trauma sometimes has detrimental effects on our ability to experience and tolerate physical intimacy with a partner. Sexual activity can feel invasive or threatening after a traumatic event, regardless of our previous comfort level because our internal alarms are still blaring. These alarms prevent us from letting our guard down, warning us away from anything that even resembles a memory of feeling vulnerable or violated. Particular touches and other aspects of sexual activity may trigger us unexpectedly or incite the terror of a flashback. For these and other reasons, surviving a sexual assault (and sometimes trauma of other kinds) often results in a decreased libido. This may also be caused or compounded by the impact of sexual side effects common to psychotropic medications (Borg & Chavez, 2014). These problems can create strain even in the best of relationships. They leave us feeling betrayed by our own minds and bodies and leave our partners worrying that we're no longer attracted to them. This is one area in particular where more education to loved ones would be helpful because the effects of trauma on our ability to experience intimacy can happen regardless of how much love, commitment, or devotion we feel toward a partner.

Trauma can also affect our ability to establish new relationships and influence the kinds of relationships that we find ourselves in. Difficulty trusting others and an overactive sense of danger present some tricky obstacles when it comes to meeting new people. And if we maintain beliefs that our traumatic experiences are our fault or that we're not good enough or that we're damaged goods, we may find ourselves settling for and even gravitating toward a pattern of relationships with partners that treat us exactly that way.

When we've survived abusive relationships (in family or otherwise), we often grow to feel uncomfortable accepting support or compliments. We may feel fully capable of giving honest, beautiful, unfiltered truth to others about how wonderful they are but recoil when sincere praise is offered back to us. We might feel selfish when asking for favors of basic courtesy or guilty when setting reasonable limits and boundaries. These patterns of self-deprecation are made to be broken. We don't benefit ourselves or anyone else from denying ourselves the respect and appreciation we offer so freely to the people we love. If we catch ourselves living by this double standard, we would do well to consider where it originated and practice living outside of its rules. Healthy relationships offer a perfect opportunity to exercise these important changes.

The quality of our relationships affects our ability to quell the severity of our trauma symptoms, and the speed of our recovery, in one direction or the other. Particularly unhealthy relationships perpetuate elevated levels of distress, paving the way for setbacks and exacerbated symptoms. Abusive relationships create patterns of retraumatization, sometimes bringing aspects of recovery to a veritable standstill until we escape. And positive, supportive relationships are by far one of the strongest assets that we can be lucky enough to have. Healthy relationships require the risk of vulnerability. Being vulnerable means being courageous enough to share our pain with another person, trusting that love and a deeper understanding of our value will come out the other side. This requires a great amount of bravery and, as we practice it, multiple leaps of faith on our part. We vitalize our recovery wonderfully when we open ourselves to connection, provided there's at least one good relationship in our lives to reciprocate it.

No relationship is expected to be perfect, but if it's rooted in patience, love, and an eagerness to learn and to take part in our healing, that support creates a powerful foundation for recovery. Our prognosis will flourish all the more from it. If we don't have healthy family or social relationships in our lives, it's all the more crucial that we develop a support system to gain and then build upon these benefits. This can start by practicing trust with good professional supports. It can begin with connecting and relating in support groups with others who have experienced trauma. It can take root by forming a trusting bond with a pet or support animal. It can't be emphasized enough that the support of family, partners, and friends is an invaluable resource and gives a pivotal advantage to those of us fortunate enough to have it.

12. What is it like to experience a flashback?

A flashback is very different from simply having a memory. In explaining what a flashback feels like, it may be useful to first briefly distinguish between normal and traumatic memory and to understand how a flashback is different from being reminded of trauma, feeling triggered, or having intrusive memories while still grounded in the present.

In a normal memory process, when we choose to recall something we've experienced, or we're reminded of some aspect of it, we tend to find our memories to be well within our control. We decide what we want to highlight in conversation and how much we want to dwell on the memory before we're done with it. When we're ready to move on, the memory reconsolidates, returning to the background where it's stored. Trauma memories, particularly when they're unprocessed and haven't yet been unified into a chronological account, tend to be less orderly, and they aren't restrained by those same predictable rules. They're scattered: at times partial and blurry and at other times very clear. They can be out of sequence and charged with emotion. They become associated with anxiety and a visceral avoidance response. Thinking or talking about them feels scary and wrong. While drawing upon these memories can be very stressful in itself, it can be equally challenging to file them back away. Once the memory's open and in the forefront of our minds, getting it back into the box and moving on with our thought process can be an arduous task.

Another unfortunate characteristic of trauma memories is that they have a habit of coming forward uninvited, suddenly, and without warning. They break through and intrude into our minds, either in reaction to a trigger or appearing to come out of nowhere. To be "triggered" means to have an anxiety response incited by an internal or external reminder of a traumatic event, often accompanied by memories, sensations, perceptions, and/or emotions associated with what happened. The intensity of intrusive symptoms falls on a spectrum from mild to severe. On the low end of that spectrum, there may be a quick image racing across our minds or an auditory memory of spoken words. On the high end, it can feel like we've left our present surroundings completely and are experiencing the trauma like it's happening again. While the exact definition of a flashback may vary a bit in academic and professional circles, it's generally agreed that a flashback would fall at the severe end of this spectrum. It involves a perceived reliving of one or more aspects of a traumatic event, as though it's recurring in the here and now. The past and the present no longer feel like two separate experiences.

Take the example of someone who's been in a car accident and is now riding as a passenger in a different vehicle. If a flashback were to happen, it wouldn't feel like just a passing and unpleasant memory of the accident. It would be more of an abrupt and very convincing feeling that the passenger is back in that original car as it's crashing. This could take the form of a visual perception of the car crash: like watching a movie in your mind and feeling like you're in the middle of it. It could also involve the passenger seeing the actual dashboard of the present car and the view out the windshield—but feeling convinced that it's a completely different place at a different time, in the original car, with the crash about to happen. The passenger's vision and hearing may highlight similar sights and sounds that correspond with what was seen and heard during the trauma (the same bright sky, the sound of the car radio, the trees passing quickly by), making it all the more convincing that it's happening all over again. Flashbacks can be triggered by any of the five senses and can manifest through all five of them as well. Veterans may perceive the smell of blood or diesel fuel when experiencing a flashback. A survivor of severe abuse at the hands of a parent might perceive verbal messages in the mind spoken in the parent's voice. It's also possible to wake up to a flashback, perhaps if triggered by a nightmare. Survivors may awaken, believing momentarily that they're back in the place of the trauma, and feel panicked and confused as they struggle to get their bearings.

Flashbacks are specifically a trauma-based phenomenon. In other words, we don't have flashbacks to everyday, routine events. We don't become engulfed and lose ourselves in positive and wholesome memories, believing they're happening again in the moment. Researchers have tried to figure out what exactly happens in the brain when a flashback occurs, for the purpose of better understanding the symptoms and informing our efforts to alleviate them. They've found that it involves a distinctly different memory process from how we would recall memories normally in that flashbacks and intrusive memories are, by nature, involuntary and uncontrollable (Brewin, 2014). Flashbacks activate certain parts of the brain but don't involve the parts that would allow us to distinguish what's happening now from what's happened in the past. When they're severe, they can bring a complete loss of this awareness, giving us the impression (and the appearance to witnesses) that we're literally reliving the trauma again (Ehlers, Hackmann, & Michael, 2004). We've also learned that flashbacks activate the right hemisphere of the brain (which is nonverbal and registers and processes emotions) but don't involve the left hemisphere (which allows for language and the opportunity to translate memories into an understandable narrative). This makes it difficult to express to others what's happening in the moment and to process and make sense of it ourselves (Lanius et al., 2004).

This may lend some explanation as to why some of the modern treatments for trauma help in alleviating flashbacks along with other trauma symptoms. Several of these treatments involve an intentional activation of the lingual, narrative part of the brain while simultaneously regulating distress and accessing traumatic memories, and one in particular, EMDR, includes intentional stimulation of both sides of the brain while processing trauma.

13. Sometimes I feel like I become numb and go distant into my head. I feel no emotions at all. What's happening to me?

This is a common and very sophisticated defense mechanism that activates with no conscious choice or effort on our part. It's called "dissociation" and happens when the brain seeks to alleviate distress by distancing perceptions and feelings from our conscious awareness. This can feel like a barrier has formed between ourselves and the outside world, as though we're covered with layers of protective numbness that prevent access to our emotions, stress, and physical sensations. If someone speaks to us or touches us, it may seem like it's coming from far away or like we're watching it happen to another person instead of ourselves. Sometimes it's an odd feeling that we're somehow existing outside of ourselves (an experience called "depersonalization") or that our surroundings are not authentic: far in the distance or otherwise distorted from how we'd normally perceive them (referred to as "derealization"). Dissociative symptoms range from mild to severe and can have effects on consciousness, memory, and our sense of identity (Greenberg, Brooks, & Dunn, 2015).

If you ask people who are dissociated what they're feeling in the moment, you'll often get a response of "Nothing." This makes sense because if their brains are trying to be protective by pushing their emotions to the background, a response of "Nothing" would be a sign of its success. When we're dissociated, we're prevented from understanding the sensations that drive body discomfort, how they're otherwise activated by triggers, and the lessons in recovery that can only be learned when our emotions can be properly identified and felt. It's very challenging to explore our inner experiences, or even to have a sense of self, when our brains have us floating in sensory deprivation for the sake of keeping us safe.

Dissociation can begin while a trauma is occurring, or it may start to manifest after the traumatic situation has passed. Survivors often recall that they had a sense of rising out of their body while an assault was happening to them, or feeling like they were watching from another corner of the room. Whether or not we dissociate at the time of a trauma may have some bearing on how we experience PTSD later on. Studies have shown that someone who has a severe dissociative response at the time of the traumatic event is more likely to be faced with relatively severe symptoms of PTSD afterward (Carlson, Dalenberg, & McDade-Montez, 2012).

Treatment of dissociative symptoms often involves teaching survivors how to "ground" themselves back into a sense of presence in mind and body. Grounding most often involves exercises that employ one or more of the five senses, such as naming colors in our line of sight, mindfully listening to music (sometimes sharpening our focus to one single instrument in a song or instrumental piece), stomping our feet or clapping our hands, or touching different surfaces with an intentional awareness, describing the sensations to ourselves as though we're feeling them for the first time. It can be achieved through aromatherapy or becoming mindfully present with the taste of a fruit or a warm cup of tea or coffee. Grounding can sometimes be more effective when two or more senses are engaged at the same time (like rubbing our hands with lotion while holding them up to our nose to take in the scent). The five senses are readily available tools that can be used to direct ourselves back to presence and to reorient to where our bodies are in relation to everything around us.

Grounding can come with some risk, as it brings the possibility of accessing at least some of the stress, memory, or emotion that the brain was trying to protect us from. This means we might feel a rise in anxiety as our dissociative symptoms lift. It's helpful to have support and some reliable anxiety management strategies at the ready for when this happens. Survivors who master grounding skills may still sometimes choose not to use them, opting instead to allow dissociation to wash over them and provide some temporary respite from distress. While relying upon a symptom as a means to relief may be not be considered ideal, there's still a lot to be said for gaining control over when it happens. What matters is that we learn to tolerate a state of presence at a pace that works for us. That tolerance lengthens with practice and strengthens as we otherwise develop resilience.

Alexithymia, which involves difficulty perceiving and identifying emotions in ourselves and others, is another possible reason why a survivor may feel "no emotions at all." Alexithymia differs from dissociation in that it can persist even when we're fully present and grounded. Treatment of alexithymia involves learning how different emotions are felt and expressed in our minds and bodies and how to recognize those emotions in the facial expressions and mannerisms of others.

14. What is borderline personality disorder, and how does it relate to trauma?

Personality development sets its foundation during our experiences in early childhood. It's during that time that we gain a fundamental understanding about who we are, primarily from how we bond and interact with our attachment figures (parents or caregivers). This is when we find out what "home life" means and when we get a first impression of our place in the world. We start to develop a sense of identity and figure out how to relate to other people. We gain deep-seated convictions about our value and how relationships are supposed to work. We discover the existence and limitations of our self-efficacy, including our capability for both resolving problems and tolerating when we don't have the power to change them. It's during our early development that we start to explore our own emotions, discern what they mean, and develop skills for regulating them in times of distress. As we grow into teenagers and adults, these qualities take root and become established patterns, setting the context for how we think and behave.

When those developed patterns are particularly maladaptive, they compromise our ability to function effectively in relationships. They undermine our capacity to succeed in school and work environments. Their collective traits vary in severity and presentation and are differentiated and defined diagnostically as personality disorders.

The *Diagnostic Manual of Mental Disorders*, fifth edition, identifies 10 uniquely defined personality disorders and outlines the common symptoms for each of them (American Psychiatric Association, 2013). Borderline personality disorder (BPD) stands out in its relation to trauma because of its theoretical underpinnings in early childhood abuse and neglect, its prevalence in our society, and the extreme suffering that it brings. The condition is called "borderline" because, in the origin of when it was first identified and studied, it was believed to be a personality that developed "on the border" between other conditions diagnosed at the time, including what was referred to as neurosis (chronic anxiety, mood problems, or emotional distress) and psychosis (loss of touch with reality, accompanied by hallucinations or delusions) (Stone, 1977).

There is some disagreement in research and in the field of mental health as to whether BPD definitively originates from developmental trauma. While it often (but not always) does correlate with significant trauma history and a concurrent diagnosis of PTSD, there are rival theories that offer valid arguments and evidence for other possible origins (Harvard Health Publishing, 2006). The answer to this question is offered with a description of BPD, as it's theorized to be originated or exacerbated by factors of trauma and resilience.

When our developmental years are marked by abuse, neglect, and invalidation, our process of self-discovery and personality development can be stifled. Survival skills are developed not from the discovery of capability, strength, and confidence but instead from a foundation of internal emptiness and fear. When our natural childhood emotions are categorically dismissed or punished, we become deprived of a crucial developmental opportunity to learn what those feelings mean and how to control them. Boundaries that would normally develop between the felt-states of safety and crisis, between where our identities end and another person's begins, and between conflicting emotion states don't have the chance to conclusively form. The chaos and confusion that fills those empty spaces become encoded into our concept of self. Unmet needs translate into deep-seated beliefs about how to ensure our survival in the dangerous world we know. The effects of these wounds become most visible in our behavior toward other people as we grow up, most notably in how we seek to get our needs met in relationships. The resulting problems can severely complicate our efforts to relate and function in society, or they can explicitly preclude any chances of doing so.

BPD is characterized by difficulty establishing a sense of one's own identity, an internal feeling of emptiness, a high level of emotional reactivity, and moods that are prone to sudden shifts, especially in reaction to heightened stress. Like any other entity of symptoms, it falls on a spectrum from relatively mild symptoms (or a situation in which someone has "traits" but not enough of them to justify a full diagnosis) to severe symptoms. In day-to-day life, BPD can feel like having a very thin skin emotionally and, beneath that, a volcanic reservoir of emotional pain and distress bubbling beneath the surface. When that reservoir is ignited, the reaction can feel instantaneous and bring waves of anger, despair, and anxiety that feel drastic and earth-shattering in the moment. Because regulatory skills and inner boundaries haven't had a chance to develop, these episodes of emotional suffering can be very difficult to contain. They spike rapidly in intensity and then take a long time to settle back down. BPD survivors may also experience dissociation or episodes of paranoia in times of elevated distress.

One common symptom of BPD is an ongoing fear of being abandoned by our partners, professional supports, friends, and family. Another is a fluctuation between the exaggerated extremes of inflating the value of people in our lives and, at other times, undervaluing and rejecting them as not good enough. This is because, like other conditions related to trauma or depression (see question 8), BPD can generate a very black-and-white way of seeing things. We're either loved or we're invalidated. We're either good or we're terrible. Our relationships are either perfect or unacceptable. There is little emotional awareness of the in-between. The gray area separating these extremes feels nonexistent.

With this binary thinking, fear of being deserted, impulsive reactivity, and difficulty tolerating distress, maintaining relationships can be extremely difficult. Survivors' understandable and deeply rooted longing for their suffering to be acknowledged and validated may be expressed through extreme and irrational behaviors. The security and boundaries of relationships are repeatedly tested because they're not otherwise felt and understood. Help may be asked for and then angrily refused. Loved ones are pushed away and tested against the expectation of abandonment, either directly or indirectly, and challenged to prove that they won't leave (or perhaps, more to the point, to prove that an already established pattern of emotional neglect and abandonment in life won't be replicated again). An internal state of emotional chaos becomes repeatedly mirrored by external crisis. There is a terrible irony in this, in that repeatedly pushing and testing relationships for validation and reassurance comes at the expense of wearing those relationships thin until abandonment becomes more likely. This is not to say that relationships will necessarily fail if one or both partners have BPD, but these symptoms can create a tragic cycle of self-fulfilling prophecy that repeats itself all too frequently.

Severe pain will often result in extreme measures of coping. Reckless and self-destructive behaviors are common with BPD, as are suicidal thoughts, attempts, and gestures. In the absence of healthier means of coping, self-harm, including cutting or burning oneself, is a tactic commonly discovered and utilized by people with BPD as a means of achieving temporary relief from emotional tension. This comes at the high cost of scars, risk of infection, and, in some cases, an addictive dependence on the practice.

The collective symptoms of BPD make it difficult to maintain the emotional regulation necessary to keep a job, to complete a college program, and, sometimes, to stay out of the hospital. The National Institute of Mental Health has reported that approximately 1.4 percent of people in the United States have BPD ("Personality Disorders," n.d.). Studies have shown that this population represents up to 20 percent of those who receive inpatient psychiatric treatment and that up to 10 percent of people with BPD ultimately commit suicide. That rate is 50 times greater than the general population (Crowell, Beauchaine, & Linehan, 2009).

Not everyone who grows up in an abusive or neglectful environment develops a personality disorder, which raises the question as to why it would happen with some survivors but not others. The origin of BPD has several theoretical components, and not all of them are environmentally or relationally caused. Marsha Linehan, PhD, a psychologist who is widely known and respected for her expertise in borderline personality disorder and treatment of it, offered a biosocial theory for the cause of BPD. In her seminal book, *Cognitive-Behavioral Treatment of Borderline Personality Disorder*, she theorized that BPD develops from a combination of biological vulnerability and chronic exposure to a dysfunctional traumatic environment in development (Linehan, 1993). Research referenced by the National Institute of Mental Health has shown possible structural and functional changes in the brain that could explain why people with BPD have such difficulty with impulsivity and dysregulated emotions, but it's not yet clear whether those differences in the brain are the cause of BPD or a result of it ("Borderline Personality Disorder," n.d.). Studies have also suggested that there appears to be a clear genetic component and biological predisposition not only for BPD but for all ten personality disorders specified in the *DSM–5* (Reichborn-Kjennerud, 2010).

When we're biologically vulnerable and raised in environments where our feelings are dismissed, shamed, ridiculed, and ignored, there can be critical consequences, both in childhood and later in life. A traumatic pattern of invalidation in development suffocates a natural process by which we learn how to identify, express, and gauge the validity of our own emotions. This renders us unequipped to keep our emotions regulated and controlled. Until we learn the skills to do so, we rely upon the strategies that we know. This is the theoretical understanding of how traumatic experiences in development may contribute to borderline personality disorder. Common treatments for BPD involve establishing an anchoring point of mindfulness from which to observe and gain insight, and developing skills to improve and master both symptom management and the healthy maintenance of relationships. Please see question 43 for more details.

15. What harmful coping mechanisms do people use to deal with trauma?

Harmful coping mechanisms for trauma are survivors' attempts to escape, mitigate, or assume some semblance of control over anxiety or emotional distress. For some, this means doing what they can to keep their worlds confined. Survivors may isolate to their homes or adhere to rigid daily routines and leave phone calls or texts from friends unanswered. They may strive to minimize human interaction by staying in touch with only one or two trusted others (sometimes only professional supports) and only go out into the community when it's absolutely necessary. They may stay up through the night and sleep during the day, preferring the relative feeling of safety when there's daylight and more sounds or activity in the home. Survivors may go to stores only during the first few minutes after they open or just a few minutes before they close, socialize online only, or use the distraction of television, the internet, or video games to burn through the hours of the day.

It would be fair to question how these strategies could be considered harmful when they don't directly hurt the survivor or anyone else. The answer would lie in the purpose served by these choices and what we sacrifice by maintaining them. Each of these coping mechanisms embraces avoidance, which brings short-term relief at a longer-term cost. When we retreat into the sanctuary of disengagement from life and social connection, it only becomes scarier and more intimidating when we entertain the thought of eventually leaving it. If we cocoon ourselves into isolation, our resolve to step outside of the cocoon diminishes over time. We reclaim that resolve by pressing against the walls of that comfort zone and ultimately breaking through to rejoin life on the outside.

Other coping mechanisms are equally seductive but more explicitly dangerous. They happen more when a survivor is at one end of the spectrum between feeling too numb or feeling too emotionally activated and equate to an immediate grab for the opposite end of what the survivor is experiencing. Survivors will sometimes resort to cutting, burning, or scratching themselves for the sake of momentary relief from emotional distress. This strategy is harmful beyond causing immediate and lasting damage to skin and the risk of infection; it fosters reliance on self-injury in lieu of healthier grounding or coping skills. Self-harm can hold allure for some as a "quick fix" in the moment, but it's also an investment in self-destruction as a tool for controlling emotional pain. It's very hard to challenge the beliefs that attack or blame ourselves for our trauma, or to convince ourselves of our own worth, when we're inflicting damage to our bodies as a means of tolerating distress.

Survivors also rely upon strategies that transform triggers or dangerous situations into coping mechanisms by harnessing the effects of the reactions they evoke. For example, sexual-assault survivors may feel drawn to watch pornography. This may be driven in part by the mind's effort to process, through a visual reenactment, some aspect of what happened. It can also be because, on some level, the survivors know that the triggering visual may be disturbing at first but will either activate the comforting distance of dissociation or produce an adrenaline rush that gives them a brief moment of feeling *something*. Veterans may watch movies and online videos about military combat for the same reasons. When used for these purposes, either to feel or not to feel, these coping strategies don't bring the same recovery benefit as a controlled exposure for desensitization (see question 32) because they rely upon overwhelm instead of attenuating it. They create "stuck points" in recovery instead of helping survivors through them.

It should be clarified that calling these ideas out as harmful or counterproductive is not the same thing as judging survivors for turning to them. Unhealthy coping strategies happen for a reason and are almost invariably driven by an underlying emotional pain or an unmet and reasonable need that, when understood, helps the behavior make sense in context. Sometimes we gravitate to harmful coping mechanisms because we haven't yet had the opportunity to learn healthier ones or to see the consequences of our actions in perspective. Sometimes we have no idea why we're doing these things or why they keep happening. They may represent an impulsive grasp for a moment of relief when emotional pain feels unbearable. Other times they're more deliberate choices but are chosen only because they're the most familiar methods we know for managing our suffering. When our threshold for distress has been breached or exhausted over time, our choices don't necessarily gravitate to what's best for us. Our first thoughts turn to what we think might work, even if only in the here and now. This is a statement arguably more fitting to the human condition than it is to trauma specifically. It fits just as reliably as a tendency in people living with depression, anxiety, addiction, or unusually high and persistent levels of stress.

These are just some examples of unhealthy choices that can originate from the effects of trauma. Refer to question 18 for more on this topic. While substance use/addiction and risky sexual behaviors certainly also count as harmful coping mechanisms, they each warrant enough attention that they're covered as separate subjects in questions 16 and 19, respectively.

16. Does trauma increase the likelihood that someone will abuse drugs or alcohol?

Yes, it does. People living with PTSD are estimated to be three to four times more likely to develop substance-use disorders than the general population is (Morgan, 2009). Findings from the perspective of addiction research reflect this correlation as well. One study in 2010 assessed 402 men and women in residential treatment programs and found that 95 percent of them had had at least one significant traumatic event in childhood, with 18.1 percent of them reporting six or more (Wu, Schairer, Dellor, & Grella, 2010).

As mentioned in the answer to question 15, the most understandable and logical response to the symptoms of PTSD is an effort on the part of the survivor to seek ways to alleviate them. It's basic human nature to pursue relief from pain, and we'll sometimes resort to the strategies we find most easily. The more severe and long-standing the pain is, and the more desolate and isolated we feel, the more options we may find ourselves considering. When an unhealthy practice is used as a coping strategy, it becomes relied upon more regularly, particularly when we're lacking in effective alternatives and healthy relationships. Whether it comes in the form of gambling, shopping, eating, sex, pornography, alcohol, or other drugs, what begins as the discovery of a measure of relief or distraction can quickly snowball out of control.

Alcohol use and other addictive behaviors can bring a dissociative effect that allows trauma survivors to more easily manage their emotions from an artificial sense of distance (Craparo, Ardino, Gori, & Caretti, 2014). This unfortunately creates a cycle that perpetuates itself not only with the ruinous spiral of problems it can otherwise cause but also because substance use can mimic or exacerbate the same symptoms that a survivor is trying to relieve. The replicated experience of dissociation is only one example. The effects of drugs and alcohol on the function of neurotransmitters have also been found to have "rebound effects" of hyperarousal and hypervigilance, to induce depressive symptoms and anxiety, and to interfere with the processing of autobiographical memory (a crucial component in trauma recovery) (Ford & Russo, 2006).

In understanding how trauma histories lead to addictive problems, we can also refer back to what we've learned from the ACE (adverse childhood experiences) studies. Traumatic childhood experiences create an increased vulnerability to medical problems later in life (see question 10), and many of those medical conditions cause severe physical pain. The soaring rate of prescribed opiate medications for pain management in this country has culminated in a nationwide crisis. Sales of prescription opiates were found to have nearly quadrupled in the United States between 1999 and 2014 (with no overall change reported in the prevalence of pain in our population), and that rise has been matched with an increase from 1.5 to 5.9 related deaths per 100,000 people during that time (from 2000 to 2014) (Kim, Nolan, & Ti, 2017). Those rates of prescription and mortality aren't specific to trauma survivors. They're representative of our entire population. The risk of addiction in itself does not discriminate. It presents a vital danger to all of us, regardless of our backgrounds, but there are some additional factors that leave trauma survivors disproportionately threatened. Because they're more vulnerable to both painful medical conditions and more prone to addiction overall, the opiate crisis is weighted inordinately against the survival of people suffering with PTSD.

Treatment programs for addiction can make all the difference in the world. In addition to the multitude of benefits brought by traditional 12-step programs and professional counseling services, there are addiction treatment models that incorporate an additional trauma focus in their design. "Seeking Safety" is a versatile treatment approach designed by Lisa Najavits, PhD, at the Harvard Medical School and McLean Hospital. Applied both in a group format and individually, it helps survivors of all genders learn coping skills to establish safety from both addiction and trauma symptoms ("About Seeking Safety," n.d.). This approach supports survivors without the need for sharing any personal details of what happened to them (Lenz, Henesy, & Callender, 2016). The "Trauma Recovery and Empowerment Model" (TREM) is a group model specifically for women that uses skill building, psychoeducation, and social support to help with addiction and recovery from abuse (Conduent Healthy Communities Institute, n.d.). There is also a 12-week program called the "Addictions and Trauma Recovery Integration Model" that blends psychoeducation, processing, and expressive activities with a focus on improving health mentally, physically, and spiritually (Substance Abuse and Mental Health Services Administration, 2014). All of these models have established themselves very well in research for their benefit to survivors with addiction (Giordano et al., 2016).

17. Does having PTSD make someone dangerous or more likely to abuse others?

This question is complicated because there's plenty of room for unfair bias if you don't touch upon all possible aspects in answering it. The question is also valid as there are symptoms and characteristics of PTSD that, for some, express as aggressive behavior. When the sympathetic nervous system is activated, a survivor may think or behave more irrationally or impulsively at times and may have episodes of increased irritability and anger. People with PTSD are statistically more likely to use substances, and those who do will be more apt to show behavior changes related to addiction, intoxication, and withdrawal. However, the fact remains that there are countless numbers of trauma survivors with PTSD who aren't aggressive people. There are also plenty of people without PTSD who are violent.

It would be deceptively easy to contrive an argument that people with PTSD are inherently more dangerous if our perspective only came from stories of people who proved to be so. If you read about a war veteran who became violent toward his wife and children after returning home, or a perpetrator of child sexual abuse who revealed a personal history of having also been molested as a child, you'd find opportunity for a surface correlation between the trauma and the offense. If you looked for more expansive answers solely by studying groups of people who've turned out to be dangerous (what's called a "retrospective study" in research circles) and the percentage of them with trauma histories, you'd have that same opportunity. However, extrapolating from the correlation and applying it to everyone who's been traumatized would be grossly inaccurate and unfair and would create fodder for misunderstanding and discrimination. Criminal trends are valid and important, but they don't generalize as universal predictors. It would be blatantly incorrect to say that someone is dangerous just because the person has PTSD and equally wrong to say that everyone with PTSD is categorically safe.

There is evidence in research that interlinks traumatic experience with criminal behavior (Ardino, 2012). Retrospective studies of prison inmates have found correlations of past abuse of different kinds ranging widely, from a low of 9 percent to a high of 79 percent ("Early Childhood Victimization . . . ," n.d.). Questions that arise in response to findings like these are: Did the trauma responses of these people contribute to their criminal behavior? How many other possible causal factors might there have been, and which ones did they share with the remaining 21– 91 percent of inmates? If trauma was a factor, then how do we account for the innumerable survivors among us who don't go on to commit crimes?

Similar questions come up regularly in conversations about sex offenders. Most people who are sexually abused don't grow up to abuse others and would be appalled at the insinuation. But it is fair to question whether sex offenders were abused themselves and, if they were, whether the effect of their trauma was at least part of the reason they became abusive. If we had an absolute and grand, sweeping hypothesis that this was a universal fact, that sexual abuse creates sexual perpetrators, the research would cause us to take pause almost immediately because we would see that while most children who are sexually abused are female, most adults who sexually abuse children are male (Plummer & Cossins, 2018). This immediately confounds any argument for a universal link because we've run into an important second variable of gender difference. We can then ask why the distinction between genders exists, and, equally important, how many other variables might explain why some abused boys grow up to become perpetrators when the majority of them do not.

A nice foundation to start from would be an official report made to the U.S. General Accounting Office (1996), which reviewed studies to determine the likelihood that people who were sexually abused as children would become sexual abusers themselves. Contributors to the report noted that most of the research they found was retrospective, which presented the aforementioned limits in trying to get the full picture. The "prospective" studies they found (in which they followed abused children forward through life to see how they turned out) concluded that the majority of those children didn't become sex offenders. They also realized that they had to account for the substantial number of sex offenders in the studies who reported no history of having been abused themselves. In review of both kinds of study (retrospective and prospective), the report concluded that while some studies do indeed conclude that childhood sexual abuse can sometimes be a causal factor in the equation, "the experience of childhood sexual victimization is quite likely neither a necessary nor a sufficient cause of adult sexual offending" (U.S. Government Accounting Office, 1996, p. 3). The report, reasonably, questioned what additional variables might be in play: Why would any given percentage of abused children grow up to abuse others, and what protective factors prevents this from happening in the majority of them?

We could raise the same questions with regard to the percentages of children in domestic-violence households who become domestic abusers themselves, abused kids who become bullies at school, or veterans who return home and later find themselves facing charges for various crimes. The U.S. Department of Veterans Affairs Office of Research and Development published an online review of findings from the work of Dr. Andrea Finlay, a health scientist and researcher, and reported that more than half of the veterans in the criminal justice system were found to have either mental health problems or substance abuse disorders (most notably alcohol or cocaine addiction). Finlay noted the need to consider additional variables, including the possible impact of traumatic brain injuries from service. The article also reported that a large percentage of incarcerated veterans are homeless or at risk for homelessness and that many others have problems finding work and reintegrating into civilian life (Richman, 2018). This begs the questions of how much veteran addiction, crime, and incarceration could have been avoided with the provision of adequate support and treatment following discharge from the military and why that deficiency in standard and practice may exist. It's also worth noting again that retrospective studies, by virtue of their direction, are a means of learning what contributed to criminal activity after the fact. They don't accentuate the veterans who aren't violent and who haven't committed crimes and certainly don't detract from the importance of what we can learn from them as well.

The assessment of potential dangerousness is a specialized area of psychology. It is a complicated subject, worthy of more research as to how it relates to trauma and how other vulnerability factors play into things. While studies on dangerousness and its causes help greatly in educating our efforts toward crime prevention, there are many wide-scale societal benefits to be gained by studying the factors that contribute to survivors' wellness and success as well.

18. Are traumatized people more likely to find themselves in dangerous situations later in life?

Unfortunately, people living with PTSD—predominantly survivors of abuse—are found to be statistically more vulnerable and likely to experience subsequent traumas later in life. Studies using ACE questionnaires (see question 10) have shown that a survivor of childhood sexual abuse is more than three times more likely to experience sexual violence in adulthood. In fact, childhood sexual abuse has been found to be among the strongest predictors of continued victimization. One meta-analysis found that 15–79 percent of women abused sexually as children were later raped as adults (Ports, Ford, & Merrick, 2016). There are similar trends in physical and emotional abuse. A global study published by UNICEF and The Body Shop International in 2006 found that the single best predictor of adults becoming domestically abused is whether they grew up in a home where they experienced domestic violence as children. Another study found that women who were physically or sexually abused in childhood had a significantly higher risk of finding themselves in domestic violence situations (Whitfield, Anda, Dube, & Felitti, 2003).

Why would someone who has been abused be more prone to become abused again? There are many possible answers to this, and they all have one thing in common. Ultimately, the reason survivors get attacked subsequently in life is that they're repeatedly targeted and assaulted by perpetrators. The culpability for each of these trends falls entirely and deservedly upon the shoulders of the people doing the offending. That may sound obvious, but the rest of this answer will be best understood if it's considered through that context.

There are a variety of factors that increase the risk for survivors to find themselves in dangerous situations. Some of them have to do with what we've come to believe about ourselves. As human beings, we tend to replicate relationship dynamics as we go through life, particularly when we're not consciously aware of what they are and how they influence us. We feel drawn to what's familiar, especially if it matches our beliefs about how the world is, our own worth, and what we deserve. This is one way that past trauma can render us more susceptible to abusive relationships. If we've grown up believing that we're worthless or that we're incapable of making our own decisions, and we're convinced that we're to blame whenever someone else gets angry, we'll be a prime target for someone who believes those same things about us. We're less equipped to challenge and refute abusive statements expressed by someone else when our minds fully endorse those same beliefs.

On the other side of things, if survivors feel that they're being treated more lovingly than they deserve, that can feel dangerous. Safe and loving relationships require trust and vulnerability. If life has taught us never to trust anyone and to keep our walls up for the sake of survival, an invitation to drop those walls can be terrifying. If we've been accustomed to chaos from the time of childhood, situations with a lack of chaos may feel suspicious and unnerving. And if we believe that healthy people are better than we are, it's easy to feel like a fraud when we're in the company of people who regard us as equals. This creates a crossed signal in the mind whereby healthy relationships feel dangerous and dangerous relationships feel ordinary. These crossed signals evolve into patterns, and by those patterns, abusive relationships are often followed by other abusive relationships. By virtue of what survivors' suffering has already taught them and for as long as they're confined by those beliefs, they're more vulnerable to be targeted by people who would seek to take advantage of that fact.

Trauma symptoms cloud our capacity for recognizing when actual danger is present, and that confusion comes from two directions. High levels of anxiety and hypervigilance raise our sensitivity to potential risk beyond what's proportionate, and that can make the process of choosing new friends and partners incredibly complicated. When we're trying to challenge ourselves by giving people the benefit of the doubt and learning to trust again, but our inner alarms are relentlessly screeching and everyone around us feels dangerous, it can be much harder to distinguish who actually is. Spotting "wolves in sheep's clothing" is challenging enough as it is, but it becomes even harder when every sheep feels like a wolf. Dissociative symptoms and alexithymia (see question 13) also present problems but for opposite reasons. They make us feel like our alarms have gone too quiet. Think about the last time that you had a bad "gut feeling" about someone you've just met. Maybe you reacted to a menacing intonation in a person's voice or something that just felt creepy in the way someone looked at you. Or maybe you couldn't put your finger on exactly what it was but had that uncomfortable rolling feeling in your stomach that told you to keep your guard up. This is your radar system, and it's designed to detect signs of danger and warn you when it perceives a threat. You listen to your gut and make your decisions accordingly. Now imagine that you're disconnected from that radar system of the brain by a barrier of emotional numbness or that your ability to read that feeling from others is blunted or nonexistent. Imagine struggling to see any difference between whether someone likes you or means you harm. This is the predicament that survivors often find themselves in, and it makes keeping themselves out of danger all the more difficult.

Trauma survivors sometimes show more explicit patterns of risky choices and behaviors, and those patterns can be driven by symptoms as much as by choice. Prolonged episodes of dissociative symptoms can become so intolerably mind-numbing that survivors resort to impulsive, thrill-seeking behaviors for invigorating rushes of adrenaline. This can include fast and unsafe driving, spending money beyond their means, gambling, or associating with dangerous people. In assessment of the reasons and motivation behind risky behaviors, studies have taught us that they help survivors regulate their emotions and regain some control over their attention and where it's focused—attention that would otherwise be absorbed in the void of their emotional suffering (Contractor, Weiss, Dranger, Ruggero, & Armour, 2017). The adrenaline boost gives at least a brief window of access to feeling (a break from feeling too numb) for some and will enable a release of tension and distress (a respite from feeling too much) for others. Substance use is perhaps one of the most prominent examples of risky behavior as it relates to retraumatization. As mentioned previously (see question 16), trauma survivors are more prone to addiction. This brings additional perils associated with intoxication, withdrawal, and overdose as well as a raised risk of financial crisis and exposure to dangerous situations.

Risky behaviors can also take the form of trauma reenactments, which are replications of environmental or behavioral aspects of the traumatic event. Research has shown that this can happen for a variety of reasons. One theory is that reenactments are a misguided attempt to gain a sense of mastery over PTSD symptoms by returning to some dangerous facet of the situation that caused them. This can include walking in unsafe areas at night, maintaining destructive relationships, or engaging in hypersexuality (Substance Abuse and Mental Health Services Administration, 2014). Studies have indicated that this is usually an unconscious process and a trade-off of perpetuating self-blame and helplessness in exchange for short-term confidence or relief (van der Kolk, 1989). Another possibility is that reenactments occur as a result of inadvertently replicated relationship dynamics (Levy, 1998), similar to those described above.

The physiological impact of trauma raises the risk for a number of survivors to fall into destructive and dangerous patterns. This doesn't apply to everyone, and survivors aren't prisoners to these statistics. Becoming traumatized one or more times doesn't automatically mean that we're destined to become traumatized again. Every example mentioned is a pattern that can be broken. Once we've gained the insight to see what's happening, we've placed ourselves one step ahead of the cycle. The rest comes down to application of that insight by seeking and engaging with the support that we need and by learning ways to quell the interference of trauma-based influences. We rise out of these patterns and improve our safety by acquainting ourselves with our value, mitigating the effects of our symptoms, and experimenting courageously with different and healthier choices.

19. Is it true that people who have been sexually abused end up more promiscuous?

Trauma affects people differently and, for some survivors, the repercussions of abuse manifest through a change in sexual behavior. To really comprehend those effects for what they are, it's important to approach this understanding with an empathetic and nonshaming mindset. When children have been sexually abused, the confusion that's caused in their minds and bodies is sometimes expressed through inappropriate sexualized behaviors. When they're observed by parents and teachers, those behaviors are pretty recognizable as upsetting residual effects of the trauma. We see them for what they are. We don't blame or judge the child for having them. When we consider how trauma affects the sexuality of adults, our understanding clarifies when we exercise that same sensibility. Sexualized symptoms and behaviors are expressed differently at different ages, and once adulthood has been reached, they're more likely to be misinterpreted, dismissed, and stigmatized. This applies both to male and female survivors of sexual abuse. We should also bear in mind that pronounced sexual behaviors may be more recognized clinically and regarded more pejoratively in our culture with regard to women than they are to men.

While changes in sexual behavior often have causal factors originating from trauma, this association doesn't apply universally to everyone. Some survivors of sexual abuse are impacted in a very opposite way, with a drop in sexual desire or an outright aversion to sex or physical intimacy. Others find their libido and sexual behaviors to be relatively unchanged. People also generally show a wide variation in libido and sexual expression, regardless of whether they've been traumatized or not. The answers to this question relate specifically to those survivors whose sexuality has been impacted by abuse or neglect. Under those circumstances, the consequences can be significant.

Women who have been sexually abused are found in research to have an increased likelihood and higher risk for unprotected sex, an increased number of sexual partners, and prostitution (Jennings, 2004). An official report made to the U.S. General Accounting Office (1996) reviewed a study that followed children over the course of 20 years after they were sexually abused and determined that they were nearly four times more likely to have been arrested for prostitution than the control group. The researchers learned that adults who experienced childhood neglect were significantly more likely than a control group to have been arrested for prostitution as well. This correlation shows that even nonsexual traumatic experiences can afflict a survivor's sexual dynamics later in life. Studies utilizing ACE questionnaires (see question 10) determined that the more adverse childhood experiences someone has had as a child, the higher the chances are that they've had sexual intercourse earlier in adolescence (Brown, Masho, Perera, Mezuk, & Cohen, 2015).

To get a clear idea of why this is so, we can look in two directions: the impact of sexual abuse on the mind, and the interplay between those effects and the dark forces in our society that capitalize on them.

Consider how trauma influences what sexuality means to us, how we get our needs met, how we find relief from symptoms, and how we make choices in relationships. When sexual abuse creates changes in sexual behavior, these are some of the dimensions in which we can become affected. Sometimes a rise in sexualized behaviors will happen out of a desire both to claim ownership and control over something that was taken from us and to reclaim a sense of empowerment over our sexuality on terms that we decide. It may happen because we've come to believe that the act of sex has no inherent meaning or value, which could also be a reflection of how we feel about ourselves or others. Other times, it's an effort to break associations from the original trauma—to escape the horror associated with the violation of our sexuality by casting some redefinition and a sense of normalcy to it. These behaviors can be a form of trauma reenactment as well, an appeal from the unconscious to gain a sense of efficacy over experiences that resemble abuse from the past (see question 18).

Like substance abuse or other risky behaviors, hypersexuality may serve as a means of either escaping our feelings or achieving feeling where there would otherwise be an empty space. Hypersexuality is a method of thrill seeking, and thus a temporary escape from emotional suffering. It can also be how survivors find comfort through the sudden and temporary closeness of intimacy without the added responsibilities of an emotional connection or commitment that they don't yet feel ready to endure.

The reasons behind these drives may be unknown, even to ourselves. How we behave is governed in large part by the unconscious fundamentals of what we've learned about the world and how to survive in it, and our sense of value (or lack thereof) in relation to others. Our core beliefs set the direction for how we strive to get our needs met and what we will tolerate. If you have very low self-esteem accented by self-blame for what happened to you, and life has taught you that your worth to others (or chances for survival) depends on how sexual your identity is, you will have a much higher risk of abuse from people who would take advantage of that vulnerability. This is how survivors become targeted and why they're susceptible to exploitation and further trauma at the hands of sexual predators. Getting repeatedly used and treated like a sexual object reinforces the denigrating beliefs that trauma instills, creating a cycle of abuse that sustains and repeats until it's finally broken. Substance abuse and addiction compound the problem, not only because they compromise inhibitions and render us more susceptible to impulsivity and danger but also because they're some of the preferred tools of sex traffickers to trap survivors into the world of prostitution.

When we've been repeatedly singled out for sexual abuse, we can easily become convinced that the pattern must somehow be our fault. Predators are all too willing to use this leverage, rationalizing their choices and shirking responsibility for their actions by finding ways to scapegoat the people they're objectifying. This unfortunately perpetuates the problem when those people are already blaming themselves.

As survivors progress in discovering their inherent worth, their dispelling of self-blame and other trauma-based associations paves the path to reclaiming their sexuality in a healthy way. Again, what "healthy sexuality" looks like can vary according to each person's libido, values, and beliefs. The goal in treatment and recovery is simply to remove the poisonous influence of the trauma and to take some lessons from what remains.

20. What effects does trauma have on society as a whole?

Researchers have recognized both the difficulty of finding an answer to this question and the call for a consensus as to what that answer would look like. Measuring the effects of trauma on society is a daunting task. Because it's very difficult to gather and quantify how survivors' quality of life is affected on a wide aggregate scale, the preferred approach boils down to calculating the societal effects of trauma in terms of financial costs (National Collaborating Centre for Mental Health, 2005). Studies using this approach have determined that there are relatively straightforward valuations you can look at, like direct mental health care specialized to PTSD, disability claims related to trauma, and related legal expenses. Other costs are more difficult to figure out. Because trauma makes one more vulnerable to substance use, addiction, and a variety of health conditions, researchers have needed to exercise some educated guesswork as to what percentage of addiction treatment and other health-care services should be attributed to it. How many people with autoimmune disease or gastrointestinal problems wouldn't have the severity of those illnesses if they hadn't been traumatized? How do you separate those people from others who didn't have trauma or who had other, concurrent vulnerabilities along with it? They run into similar complications when they look at welfare programs for people who are unemployed, disabled, incarcerated, or homeless ("The Impact of Trauma," n.d.). There are a great many factors, and combinations of factors, that can lead to those circumstances. How many relate to trauma?

That hasn't stopped researchers from trying to formulate a general idea. The website of Unbroken Warriors (https://unbrokenwarriors.org), an organization dedicated to providing support to veterans, gives us a number to begin with by pointing out that an estimated 8 percent of Americans have PTSD, which equates to about 24.4 million people, around equal to the population of Texas. Unbroken Warriors provides statistics calculating the expenditure from anxiety disorders in general to be well over $42.3 billion (Facts about PTSD and Veterans, n.d.).

Here is what other researchers have had to say:

A research effort to estimate the overall cost of child abuse and neglect in the United States concluded that it would be $103.8 billion, at a 2007 dollar value (Wang & Holton, 2007). Another study estimated the number to be closer to $124 billion (Fang, Brown, Florence, & Mercy, 2012).

If we're calculating expenses related to incarceration, we can consider a report from the Justice Policy Institute stating that out of more than 93,000 children locked up in juvenile correctional facilities, 75–93 percent of them are estimated to have experienced some degree of trauma (Adams, 2010).

With regard to health care, it was reported in research as long ago as 1992 that survivors of abuse accessed the health-care system two to 2.5 times more often as those who weren't abused, and that nearly 17–37.5 percent of health-care dollars are spent on trauma-related costs. That translates to somewhere between $333 billion and $750 billion annually (Dolezl, McCollum, & Callahan, 2009).

Research from logistic regression models has shown that for every three additional types of trauma experienced in childhood, survivors were 53 percent more likely to be involved with the juvenile justice system, 41 percent more likely to have received services based in the school setting, 204 percent more likely to have received mental health services, 216 percent more likely to have been involved with child welfare, 25 percent more likely to have received general health-care services, and 206 percent more likely to have received intensive mental health services (Briggs et al., 2012).

It's important, of course, to get the most accurate impression possible and to register the weight of these numbers when planning for political and social intervention because educated awareness precedes informed action. As the prevalence of trauma becomes more common knowledge to the public, it opens more conversation and brings more opportunity for survivors and their families to feel less alone in their struggles. Education on a wide scale dispels ignorance and discrimination, and it catalyzes more education and understanding. This is essential because to whatever depth and for whatever duration our society is affected by trauma, we share as a community in the effects of what it deprives us of, whether we know it or not. Survivors' loved ones know all too well what we're missing: those immeasurable benefits from our loved ones' talents and gifts, their industry and creativity, the beauty of their smiles, and the peace of mind that lies buried beneath the pain and commotion of their symptoms. Those losses are incalculable and amount to a cost that could never be quantified in dollars.

The following sections address how survivors' strengths and gifts are discovered and reclaimed in the process of recovery and how they can be maintained through the learned power of resilience.

Resilience

21. What is resilience?

Resilience is the durability of our psychological constitution in stressful situations and our ability to adapt to adversity without becoming overwhelmed by it. It's the protective physiological fortitude that determines how effectively we cope in a moment of crisis and how swiftly we will recover after the crisis has passed. Resilience isn't one particular asset. It's a sum total of multiple strengths and attributes that include, among other things, our sense of personal efficacy, the faith we have in ourselves, the degree to which we feel valued and loved by others, our versatility in problem solving, and how effectively we maintain a sense of safety in the world as we understand it. It's also a measure of wellness and attunement between the mind and the body, including our awareness of somatic distress and how well we've learned to tend to it.

Resilience is an internal safeguard and our first line of defense against the effects of trauma. It enhances our chances of coming out okay once the danger has passed and we're on the other side of it. Psychological trauma burdens the mind beyond its threshold to process and metabolize what's happening. Resilience is what determines how high or low that threshold is set and how much it can be pushed before an overwhelm takes place. It's a dynamic measure, in that people with high resilience may become less resilient over time (e.g., from exposure to trauma or compromised wellness), and people with low resilience can learn skills to raise it. For that reason, you can think of resilience as both a skill set and the protective bubble that it creates. Resilience gained will speed the process of recovery, and the process of recovery will build resilience.

A high degree of resilience doesn't mean that we will never become frazzled or stressed. It doesn't automatically grant us immunity from becoming traumatized by any particular adverse event. But it does certainly stack the deck in our favor by both mitigating the damage caused and lessening the time it takes to regain our sense of safety. To be resilient doesn't mean that we become dismissive of horrible things that have happened to us. It isn't found by closing ourselves off to our emotions or by isolating from connection with others. It's gained when we're brave enough to show vulnerability, both to others, when we need to ask for help, and to ourselves, when we're taking accountability for our choices. Resilience is not false hope. It's not achieved by staying in unhealthy situations but is what helps us survive and escape them. It's found in the parts of ourselves that we hold onto for as long as we're stuck in abusive relationships or traumatic situations and that propel us toward change when it becomes possible.

While some people may seem reliably resilient in the face of crisis, and others generally less so, resilience isn't necessarily uniform in any of us. We can become remarkably skillful and adaptable in handling some types of stressors but still find ourselves quickly overwhelmed by others. Someone who handles work pressure exceptionally well may falter regularly when faced with relationship stress, or vice versa. We often have the least resilience in those areas of life where past trauma afflicts us the most. It can be improved and strengthened in a general sense, and we can also devote our attention and build resilience in the context of specific situations. It's a matter of skill building, in tolerating and rising above distress. It's the learned ability to control impulses, to discover and strengthen our willpower, and to consult with our emotions without being carried away by them. It's the practice of creativity and flexibility in problem solving and patience with ourselves in the process. Perhaps above all else, resilience is the practice of not giving up. If we have given up, resilience is found in the act of starting again.

22. What factors contribute to resilience?

Like trauma, resilience can be found and defined by its presence across four dimensions: the mind, the brain, the body, and our relationships. There's a generous interplay shared between the four areas because when resilience is developed in any one of them, it complements its growth in the other three.

Resilience in the mind depends on many factors, including the confidence we feel in our value and potential as human beings and how safe and secure we feel in the world around us. We benefit from the strength of our self-esteem, our self-efficacy, and our ability to tolerate emotional distress. These qualities are among the most commonly damaged and depleted by the effects of trauma, and as they're discovered or reclaimed, they become foundational keystones in resilience development.

We contribute to mental resilience by challenging ourselves with incremental steps toward our goals in life and in recovery and by proving our capabilities as we move forward. We cultivate it through our setbacks as well as our successes. Setbacks show us when to adjust our approach. They teach us to tolerate vulnerability and to ask for support from others when we need it. They provide opportunity to develop more versatility in problem solving. Successes educate us about our aptitudes and help us trust that we can rely upon them. As we build upon our sense of self-worth and become more skillful in managing distress, we strengthen our capacity for handling even tougher challenges. We become slower to overwhelm when we're facing them. This is how we recover what's been lost and, sometimes, how we find abilities that we never knew we had.

Improved resilience is encoded into the brain through the power of neuroplasticity. The habits and trends that we develop in our thinking are changed and maintained on a cellular level in the brain, which informs how we perceive and respond to future situations. As we learn and practice new ways to cope when we encounter crisis, and we come to recognize our own potential, our brains mainstream these empowered beliefs into new neural pathways. Healthier and more accurate perspectives are consolidated and reinforced with each lesson learned and every successful step taken toward recovery. Reactive thoughts that once lowered resilience are replaced by more functional ones, and the fear-based negativity bias instilled by trauma gradually shifts into something much more balanced and workable.

As our worldviews transform from fear to safety, from helplessness to self-reliance, and from overwhelm to acceptance, our brains keep the tally of these changes and register them as a representation of the new "normal." When these changes are combined with wellness, relaxation, and a mindful relationship with the body, stress hormones are no longer activated and released with such frequency. This means that the brain idles with less distress and more tranquility. It becomes much less likely to blow a fuse and resort to dissociation. A more resilient brain has a greater neurological capacity to problem-solve, and it neutralizes stress more rapidly and more efficiently.

Resilience in the body is advanced with adequate sleep, nutrition, hydration, sobriety, exercise, self-care, and interoception. It is depleted by the lack of these things. Interoception is a concept that's been gaining more attention in the study of trauma and is defined in research as our perception of what is happening in our bodies, including how our bodies register stress and emotion (Ceunen, Vlaeyen, & Van Diest, 2016). We feel emotion physically when our hearts are broken. We feel it when we're afraid and just as much when we're loved and happy. Following trauma, we retain the visceral remnants of the fear that we felt (or still do feel) as well as the somatic sensations of sadness, anger, and shame. If we've been physically or sexually violated, the sense of safety in our bodies can feel like it's been stolen. We may feel betrayed by how our bodies reacted, or didn't react, in a traumatic encounter. A traumatized brain will sometimes cope with these problems by cutting off awareness of our sensations or misinterpreting them as strictly bodily perceptions that aren't related to underlying mental suffering. Just as trauma mutes the communication between our bodies and our minds, resilience is developed from bringing that communication back online. This can be intensely challenging for some survivors. The process needs to be paced very deliberately and in accordance with each person's readiness and ability. Developing our interoception can bring incredible benefit in building resilience and progressing our recovery. This is how we learn to tolerate and gain insight from what we feel. We introduce or regain access to a somatic perception of inner safety and take ownership of our bodies back into our awareness.

Our success in developing resilience is also determined in large part by our relationships with the people in our lives. Research into the predictors of resilience has evaluated different variables like age, medical health, education, degree of trauma exposure, and socioeconomic status, among other things. It has found social support to be one of our strongest assets (Bonanno, Galea, Bucciarelli, & Vlahov, 2007). The foundation of our resilience is typically established developmentally during our early childhood experiences. To whatever degree we grew up with loving attachment figures, had our worth validated and our talents nurtured, and lived in a safe environment, our resilience was granted strong roots and a head start. If we weren't lucky enough to have these kinds of relationships in our early lives, we can still gain resilience by finding them. Supportive relationships arm us with more deeply ingrained feelings of safety, competence, and security. Once we know that we have people who love us and have our back in rough times, we learn to know our value even when life pushes us to question it. When we have dependable people from whom we can seek wise counsel, we learn how not to feel alone even when we are. It's never too late to introduce ourselves to healthy relationships and to learn how to reinforce ourselves with the vital resilience benefits that they provide.

23. Can resilience be learned and improved upon?

Absolutely. Across all dimensions where resilience can reside, we have opportunities to build upon it. The more resilience we create, the higher our capacity to manage crisis before we reach the point of psychological overload. First and foremost, resilience is improved upon when we've tended to the trauma that we already carry. Recovery from a traumatic event or series of events doesn't always require professional intervention, but if you live with moderate to severe symptoms, specialized mental health treatment can make all the difference in the world. Resolving existing trauma not only helps alleviate symptoms but also awards us dividends in the development of resilience along the way. See "Treatment Options and Recovery" for a discussion about setting a path for recovery and a review of some of the most effective treatment interventions.

When some people think of "being resilient," they associate it with stuffing their feelings and "white-knuckling" their way through stressful situations. While there is arguably some fleeting worth in that tactic, to the extent that it functionally gets us through tough moments, it's an endurance of suffering at our own expense. When we find ourselves agonizing beforehand or exhausted afterward, these are signs that there are stronger and much easier states of resilience yet to be discovered. We access them as we resist the urge to bury or avoid how we feel, glean insight from those emotions, and learn how to mitigate our responses to distress, in body and in mind.

A focused mind-body connection allows us to tune into the emotional charge that's encrypted through our nervous systems. We can learn a great deal from the feelings that radiate within us when we're reminded of trauma or try to think or talk about it. But we first need to learn how to access and tolerate these feelings without reaching the point of overwhelm. Researchers in the field of traumatology have explained that by simply learning how to achieve relaxation in the body, particularly where our stress and emotions are felt, we can reduce the severity of our symptoms of trauma. They've learned that if we expand upon that skill, by learning to relax those same areas when faced with stressful or triggering situations (a concept called "reciprocal inhibition"), we're rewarded with a reduction in stress response and an increase in resilience (Gentry, Baranowsky, & Rhoton, 2017). There are many strategies that can help us become more skillful in achieving body relaxation, including mindfulness, aerobic exercise, yoga, progressive relaxation routines, muscle tension and relaxation exercises, specialized somatic psychotherapies, and specific breathing techniques. The process of tending to our mind-body connection can be uncomfortable or triggering at first, especially when our bodies don't feel like they completely belong to us anymore or we don't feel any sense of sanctuary in our own skin. Resilience thrives when we learn to approach those sensations in a controlled way, to access and release the emotions behind them, and to introduce relaxed sensations where fear and tension were once held. Pacing is extremely important, and there are trauma-informed therapy approaches specifically suited to help with this process.

In an article published online, traumatologists Anna Baranowsky, PhD, and J. Eric Gentry, PhD, LMHC, explained that by relaxing the muscle groups that carry this tension, the body moves away from sympathetic dominance, which in turn improves our neocortical functioning. This elevates our abilities to practice good judgment and reasoning, to control our impulses, to connect with others, and to be more deliberate and thoughtful in our decisions (Gentry & Baranowsky, 2013). This means that a wonderful reciprocal loop of resilience is created by which a relaxed body better equips the mind that is learning how to better relax it. As our sympathetic nervous systems become less activated, we become more physiologically capable to problem-solve on a more complex level as opposed to the less-strategic black-and-white solutions that we may resort to in a moment of panic. Hypervigilance calms and gives way to an unfettered awareness, opening an increased capacity for focused thought and sound judgment. By establishing some psychological distance from impulsive or fear-based reactions, we're granted the time and space to be more deliberate, strategic, and successful in our management of stressful situations. It becomes easier to consider our options in response to a crisis, to weigh the pros and cons of each, and to plan a course of action. We develop our ability to distinguish between the problems we have control over and those we do not, which is a central resilience skill in itself.

We also enhance our resilience when we become more mindful of our reactive thoughts and beliefs and correct the distortions that past painful experiences have taught us to believe. This means not only challenging and modifying the beliefs that don't serve us but also cultivating an awareness of the love and beauty that can be found in our lives. Living in survival mode can easily blind us to these things over time until we become doubtful that they even exist. It is possible to shift and dismantle our internal certainty that the world is awful, dangerous, and unloving, and it's of vital importance that we do so. That is where restorative peace of mind is to be found. The process of challenging our fear-based world-views and gathering proof that real safety can actually be felt informs our appeal to a sympathetic dominant nervous system that it's finally okay to relax. We accomplish this by mindfully connecting with evidence of what is safe, what is trustworthy, what is innocent, what is joyful, what is numinous, and what is beautiful in the world we live in. This doesn't mean briefly noticing these things in a half-hearted way just to say that we did it. It means taking the time to be present, and absorbing the fact that they're real and that they're here. It means deepening our awareness of them until we feel it, again and again, much like we previously learned to do with sources of anxiety and fear. The neuropsychologist Rick Hanson and neurologist Richard Mendius described this process beautifully in their book *Buddha's Brain: The Practical Neuroscience of Happiness, Love & Wisdom*. They explained that by the deceptively simple exercise of becoming aware of the beauty that our minds automatically filter out (an exercise they call "taking in the good"), we can counter the negativity bias in our perceived worlds and change the neural landscape of our minds in the process (Hanson & Mendius, 2009, p. 67). We benefit from the regular exercise of focused mindfulness and gratitude, and all the more so when they're practiced deliberately and frequently. For some, this practice is supplemented by a spiritual belief in a higher power, whether defined and understood through the context of organized religion or otherwise.

Finally, one of the most important ways we can improve upon our resilience is to come out of our shells and learn to trust people who deserve to be trusted. Resilience is fostered when we have the courage to reach out for a helping hand and when we acknowledge to ourselves that we're worth the effort. However the world has shocked us with how horrible it can be, that fallout is reduced when we form safe bonds with others. They provide opportunity to challenge our fear-based beliefs about people in general and to gain more of an understanding about ourselves. A principal framework of resilience comes from finding security in our sense of identity; by engaging in healthy relationships, we gain more of an understanding of who exactly our "self" is. We become more aware and attuned to our own value as human beings. We learn the depth and the edges of our beliefs and values and gain a basis for understanding how boundaries work. As our sense of identity strengthens, we become more likely to see times of adversity for what they are and less likely to misinterpret our injuries as personal shortcomings and reasons for shame.

24. How will I know when I've developed a strong degree of resilience?

If you've survived a traumatic event and you're at least considering the active pursuit of recovery or greater wellness, you're already demonstrating an admirable degree of resilience. If you devote yourself to practicing the kinds of skills outlined in the answers to the previous two questions (and expanded upon in the next chapter), you'll have a chance to witness progress from where you are. Resilience is measured in your responses to adversity, each and every time you're faced with it. When you find that you're slower to feel overwhelmed, more confident in welcoming challenges, and surprising yourself when you look back at your achievements (which does require giving yourself credit for them), you'll know you're really getting somewhere.

The best means of proving the strength of your resilience is by recognizing your power of choice and taking responsibility for how that power is used, regardless of whether your decisions are carrying you forward or holding you back. This doesn't mean taking responsibility for the choices of others. You're not responsible for what others have done to you. You are responsible for deciding where you go from here. Resilience won't be developed or proven through self-deprecation, guilt, isolation, or making yourself small. You won't build it by calling yourself lazy when you're exhausted or depressed, or by telling yourself that you're weak when you're emotionally injured or afraid. Resilience isn't found by internalizing negative judgment or abusive statements from others, scrutinizing the speed of your recovery against someone else's, or comparing where you are in life to people who haven't been through the same challenges. It's generated and confirmed through accountability, and you can hold yourself accountable for change and growth without invalidating any of the pain that you feel or shaming yourself for the scars that still show.

The process of building resilience, by definition, means that you're starting at a lower point and moving forward from there. Expect that you'll be tolerating times of increased stress, and be gentle and patient with yourself when those times happen. Too often, survivors believe that anticipatory anxiety, fear of change, false starts, and setbacks mean that they're not cut out to be resilient people. This couldn't be further from the truth because if you're experiencing any of these things, it means that you're either considering moving forward or you're in the active practice of doing it. Anxiety is a natural reaction to the unknown, especially when you don't yet know what you're capable of. Every step forward is a test, an accomplishment, and an act of courage, regardless of whether you feel brave in the moment that you're taking it. Remember that people who show the greatest feats of strength in trauma recovery don't tend to feel very strong at the time that they're happening. You'll know you're breaking through some important growing pains when you feel the urge to avoid healthy changes that make you anxious, you see the excuses rise in your mind as to why you shouldn't make them, and you decide to continue forward anyway. The development of resilience isn't easy, but it's accomplished more readily when you set a pace of growth that works for you. Find that speed where you're continually challenging yourself without overwhelming and shutting down. If you don't move forward by yards or feet, then move by inches. Resolve grows as it's tested. Strength begets strength. Momentum builds. Small achievements will supplement your confidence and prepare you for bigger accomplishments.

Your resilience is confirmed when you haven't given up. If you have given up, it's demonstrated by dusting yourself off, picking a direction, and starting again. This can happen at any time, at any point. It can happen as many times as it needs to. The process of recovery isn't a continuous line of improvement, with each day or week better than the last. There are ups and downs, successes and failures, all of which provide learning opportunities for tailoring your approach. Movement may slow to a crawl or halt completely, but it never ceases to be an option. It is never too late to gain resilience or to progress in recovery. Find your reasons for continuing on and hold onto them, and as you do that, allow your supports to hold onto you.

An advanced level of resilience is proven when you're faced with new challenges and you know to bet on yourself. You'll find yourself taking responsibility for what you can control and adapting more quickly to handle what you cannot. You won't be as quick to feel threatened by stress when it poses no physical danger. You'll no longer be living in a constant state of fear or suspicion. You will have the courage to reach out for support and to show vulnerability when you need to. Strong resilience comes from knowing that you're worth fighting for. It comes from a willingness to find your voice when you need to use it and to find your feet when it's time to move on, particularly when others set out to diminish you. As it flourishes, resilience awards a strength of identity and an awareness of self-value that no longer rely upon others' approval or permission for them to exist.

25. What can teachers, health-care providers, and other professions do to help improve resilience in others?

This is an excellent question because while every one of us has the ability to promote resilience development in others, there are certain professions that are exceptionally well positioned to do so. Our primary tools in fostering resilience are the gifts of our awareness, our compassion, and our devoted intervention.

Teachers, childcare workers, and school guidance counselors are uniquely qualified in this regard because they're on the front line and in direct service to one of our most vulnerable populations. They're tasked with the charge of helping our children figure out who they are, how the world works, and what the difference between right and wrong is. It's through these early interactions that kids discover what they're worth and what it means to have friends. They come to recognize their capabilities and experiment with their talents. They learn how it feels to be cared for by a safe adult. Our children depend upon us for guidance, and they take lessons from every significant adult in their lives, one way or another. These professionals accept and shoulder a great responsibility because they nourish resilience at its foundational roots. No effort to do so is wasted. In his book *David and Goliath*, author Malcolm Gladwell explained that when teachers nurture students' awareness of their abilities, it helps them to create a "self-concept." This equips children to cultivate resilience as they're faced with academic challenges. A similar benefit is awarded when students are helped to discover their abilities outside of the classroom (Gladwell's example is athletics) because a sense of identity and achievement in one area of life has been found to translate to confidence and "toughness" when enduring stress in others (Gladwell, 2013, pp. 80–91).

Many young children have already experienced abuse or other serious adverse events by the time they're in school or receiving childcare services. The signs and effects of past and ongoing trauma are sometimes easily identified and other times can go unrecognized for far too long. This isn't to say that the professionals involved in children's lives are at all blind or indifferent to these problems. They often prove to be keenly aware of warning signs for trauma and are very quick to intervene when it's discovered. It could be easily argued that school and childcare culture in the United States has set a standard for prioritizing awareness and improving the quality of intervention in recent decades. It's now much more commonplace for schools to institute zero-tolerance policies for bullying as well, with varying rates of success, and this sort of campaign can help immensely. Our current wide-scale dilemma isn't so much the lack of response when trauma is discovered. It's that too much trauma remains undiscovered. This is an area that we can still work to improve upon.

There is an extraordinary and necessary paradigm shift occurring in parts of the nation. Many schools are launching an organized initiative to become "trauma-informed." They're developing programs to educate teachers about the ACE studies (see question 10) and their implications. They're demonstrating how to recognize students' behaviors that are based in sympathetic dominance and beyond the students' ability to self-regulate. These programs introduce educators to specific skills and strategies that they can teach kids in the moment when they need to alleviate distress. They're encouraging and facilitating connection between at-risk students and the teachers they trust and bond with the most. Equally important, these trauma-informed schools are exploring new ways to increase support to the teachers themselves, with increased attention toward breaks between classes, collaboration between educators when one of them needs backup, and provision of opportunities for improved self-care and prevention of burnout.

Early intervention carries benefit that lasts across the life span. We don't need to be in any particular job position to have an impact, and the value of our guidance and care cannot be overstated. Survivors who have had at least one positive relationship with a safe, caring person, especially through early childhood development, are granted an asset that will strengthen their resilience and serve as a foothold in recovery for the rest of their lives. This is the contribution that we can give, and individual interactions ripple and generalize to societal impact. Jim LaPierre, LCSW, CCS, a dual-diagnosis clinician, author, and prolific blogger, wrote that he was once asked what could possibly turn the rising tide of addiction in our society. His answer was simple, and it applies just as beautifully to how we can maximize our impact in fostering resilience and trauma recovery in others: "Invest in every child that you meet" (LaPierre, 2019).

The benefit that we can offer in strengthening the resilience of others certainly doesn't stop with children. We never "age out" of the need for support, and there are many other professions that can make a huge difference in increasing resilience for trauma survivors. Health care is another powerful context in which to do so. Physicians, nurses, and specialists encourage resilience by spreading awareness and education about trauma and its effects, gaining a working understanding of the ACE studies and subsequent research, and using their own tools to screen for history of abuse and other vulnerability factors. These simple practices not only inform the historical context of certain medical conditions but also raise awareness of their patients' need for supplemental mental health support if they're not already receiving it. Simply acknowledging trauma and its potential to increase susceptibility to illness can have a powerful effect in validating a patient's concerns and offering some possible answers to long-standing questions. It opens conversation and brings attention to important mental health needs that may otherwise go unknown and unmet and has the added benefit of strengthening the patient's bond with and trust in the health-care providers who dare to broach the subject.

The reciprocal relationship between substance use and trauma is an equally necessary point of awareness for health-care professionals because to address one without screening for the other invites missed opportunities for intervention. Providers who adequately screen for both will be armed with a more educated sense of direction for both treatment and referral. This dramatically enhances potential for success in treatment and gives their patients a strong and sometimes early advantage as they work toward sobriety and recovery.

While resilience in the individual is compromised by trauma, the bane of resilience on a societal level is apathy. We promote resilience in others by acknowledging pain when we see it, responding with empathy, and devoting ourselves to appropriate action where it's needed. This can be done through the capacity of our professions or through our equally important roles as parents, partners, family members, colleagues, and friends.

Treatment Options and Recovery

26. How is recovery from trauma achieved?

A key launching point to recover from trauma is to first embrace the idea that it's possible. This can be much more difficult than it sounds, particularly if survivors have endured symptoms for prolonged periods of time or have found past treatment attempts to be nonproductive. People sometimes won't dare to hope that recovery is an option when it's managed to remain elusive for much of their lives. They can struggle equally with accepting the truth that they deserve it.

While recovery is defined personally by each individual survivor, it begins with a necessary component of basic safety. If we live in dangerous environments, feel unsafe toward ourselves or others, have untreated, serious medical conditions, are endangered by substance use or other addictive behavior, or don't have shelter or basic food security, these needs become the first priority. These are basic survival requirements. Recovery becomes accessible by meeting these needs and resolving these dangers first, and we don't need to tackle these problems alone. Help is available. It can be accessed through case management and crisis services, domestic violence hotlines and shelters, and other community-based resources.

Arguably equal in importance is our need for supportive and healthy relationships. When survival and social connection needs are both met, we're granted a more solid foundation to pursue relief from our symptoms and to otherwise resolve the problems in our lives that were inflicted by trauma. A sense of belonging empowers us to challenge long-held doubts about our value and potential as human beings and softens our general distrust of others. When we can freely express our fears and uncertainties with people who care about us and consider the reality checks we get in response, our worldviews begin to evolve away from the bias of trauma's influence and closer to the truth. Our perspectives gradually change shape and allow for feelings of safety and future potential, clearing our view to the reality that both of these things exist. An attempt at recovery in isolation isn't just ill-advised; it's a loaded and unnecessary deprivation that reinforces distorted beliefs that we're not good enough or safe enough to be included in the world outside our homes.

Trauma often causes a breakdown in our ability to imagine what a life after it would look like or even to conceive of having a future to begin with. It extinguishes our capacity for creativity and imagination, making it hard to consider any plans or goals beyond the immediate need to alleviate suffering. For this reason, the next priority in recovery for many survivors is finding relief from trauma-based symptoms. To that end, there's a lot we can do, and this is where the treatment modalities described in this section can help tremendously. They're designed to facilitate these changes and to support people in developing these skills.

To the extent that trauma has changed the functioning of our brains and minds, we recover by learning the skills to quiet our internal alarms, regulate our emotions, and mitigate our distress. We recover by processing and integrating the truth of our experience, at a speed and in a manner that works best for us. We work with our memories according to how they've been stored, give form to the narrative of what happened, and finally resign our stories to the past where they belong. We challenge our reactive thoughts about being unsafe, about being unlovable or not good enough, and adjust the circuitry of our worldviews until they're no longer defined by self-loathing and terror. We gain recovery in the mind by recognizing and changing those habits that are unsafe, desensitizing to what is safe, and breaking out of patterns of avoidance. We learn to stop the sanction of shame that we carried but didn't deserve. We develop resilience when confronted with stressful situations, and we practice suspending and cultivating the time between our initial reactive thoughts and our actions in response to them.

When trauma has disconnected our conscious awareness from our bodies, we learn to reconnect our awareness to the feelings and sensations that are physically harbored, and we restore or introduce visceral feelings of safety where anxiety has been held. We learn to ground ourselves from dissociation and tolerate being present. We bring relaxation to our muscles, gently guiding ourselves out of the routine activation of sympathetic dominance. We give foundational power to our recovery and resilience by embracing habits of good sleep, nutrition, hydration, exercise, and sobriety.

To whatever degree trauma has caused us to fear other human beings and lose faith in humanity, we recover by discerning where true safety can be found in the presence of others. We learn to acknowledge toxicity where it exists in our relationships and introduce necessary limits, good boundaries, and a healthy distance from people who cause us harm. We connect ourselves with supportive relationships and allow them to earn our trust, with the understanding that earning trust takes time. We learn from the experiences, pain, and successes of other survivors and supports who connect with us genuinely. We discover and build upon our understanding of our own identities as they become enriched and clarified through our interaction with others. We learn to tolerate our feelings without sedating them, and our social connections without running from them, and we refrain from trying to outdistance either with rushes of adrenaline from impulsive or unhealthy choices.

If trauma has left us with lasting physical injury or illness or irrecoverable losses, we determine and expand our recovery by recognizing what we have control over in our lives and finding peace and acceptance where we don't.

Recovery from trauma means that we're embracing an identity that isn't defined entirely by what happened to us. Aside from "someone who has been through trauma" or "someone who has PTSD," how would you describe yourself? What can you say about your interests and your strengths as a person? Don't be discouraged if you feel like you're describing who you used to be or if you simply don't know. If you have a good sense of humor, or you're smart, or you're creative or artistically talented, or you're a good friend to others—every one of those characteristics can be stifled from your awareness when trauma symptoms are flaring. You may feel uncomfortable admitting what makes you stand out because staying small and keeping invisible have been your default strategies for survival. But no matter how buried they may be, and even if you can't see them, those strengths and interests that make up your true identity do exist, and they don't belong to the trauma. They belong to you. These are parts of yourself that can be reclaimed or discovered for the first time, and sometimes that's a lot of what recovery means. They're strengthened when you experiment with what you're capable of in life and in relationships.

If you're not yet able to name them, they'll become more accessible as you work through the undeserved shame that fogs your sight. If you'd like a head start toward that end, ask healthy people in your life to describe your positive qualities. When they have answers to share, listen to them without interrupting or dismissing what they say. Allow for the safe bet that they're onto something.

Advanced recovery is achieved by designing the next leg of the journey: a new chapter of who we are and how we're moving forward in spite of what we've been through. This is where the aspects of our lives that were interrupted and frozen by the trauma finally shake free and begin moving again, when we get to design "what comes next" in our life stories. We don't need to be symptom-free for this to start because growth can happen at any time and, by definition, is meant to be a work in progress. The form of our new narrative is guided by our needs, values, and individual life goals. It might begin by learning how to set limits with others and establishing healthy boundaries in relationships. Our first major turning point may be decreasing our social isolation or starting a life of sobriety. It could be about reestablishing contact or improving relationships with parents, partners, children, or friends. We may feel driven to develop our relationship with a higher power or to draw from our experiences to help or educate others. Perhaps the most common and often recommended ingredient of recovery is some type of vocational or educational pursuit. This could be volunteering, part-time or full-time employment, or taking classes toward a GED or college degree. The reasons are self-evident. It would only make sense that self-edification and service to others would be the most direct means of advancing our own healing. They provide the most reliable opportunity for developing self-efficacy, a sense of purpose, and meaningful inclusion in the community.

The best summation to answer this question is that recovery from trauma is achieved by not giving up on it. Progress isn't linear. Even when the direction is right and the methodology is perfect, the path to recovery is marked by small steps forward, large strides forward, and setbacks of varying size, each of which awards an opportunity to learn about what carries us closer to wellness and what doesn't. Recovery is created out of the realization and celebration of the self that survived and is rising from its history as a stronger human being. The catalyst for this change sometimes comes from recognizing when we need to cut our losses from unhealthy paths that we've walked for far too long and at our own expense, and to practice stepping away from them. See questions 45 and 46 for more information about achieving recovery after trauma and figuring out what that looks like.

27. What are some of the biggest obstacles that people face in their efforts toward recovery?

Some of the biggest obstacles to recovery in trauma survivors are fear, avoidance, and the unhealthy coping strategies we use to keep that avoidance sustained. These habits anchor us to the ground and prevent forward movement. They hold us back with doubts about ourselves and dread of the unknown. They drive us to impulsive and unhealthy choices, packaged as a means to escape our suffering as quickly as possible without regard for longer-term consequences.

We can learn a lot about these obstacles and how they affect us by exploring our ambivalence in taking steps toward recovery. Ambivalence is the state of uncertainty and procrastination that we feel when we're considering or making changes that contribute to our growth. It happens when one part of us knows that we'd be healthier or more successful if we did something differently and another part of us rushes to find every argument why we shouldn't do it. Ambivalence isn't an obstacle to recovery in itself so much as it is a measure of our readiness for change. It's uncomfortable to consider leaving the familiarity of what we've become accustomed to, even when what we're accustomed to isn't meeting our needs. As we consider taking steps toward necessary changes, we'll often bounce back and forth between ambivalence and motivation, between feeling stuck and feeling hopeful, while we weigh our dissatisfaction with the status quo against the discomfort of doing something differently. Most change doesn't happen instantly, like flipping a switch. It happens only after we've explored our pros and cons for making it happen, found our own reasons, marshaled our courage, and finally stepped into action. Our motivation swells and fades and then swells again, swinging back and forth until we accumulate the momentum to keep moving in the right direction.

When someone is living with symptoms of PTSD or an addiction, there are some important additional factors to consider. Post-traumatic symptoms and addictive behavior both bring intense suffering and at the same time compel us to avoid change. They deplete our resolve and train us to doubt our own capability. They convince us that we're not strong enough or worthy enough to trust and show vulnerability to others. Fear will paralyze our best intentions, and our minds will react to it by searching for reasons why we shouldn't take steps to become healthier (otherwise known as "secondary gains") or by consciously or unconsciously sabotaging our own efforts.

Secondary gains are the often-unspoken reasons "not to get well." They originate in the fear of change that would come from recovery. They come from the assumption that if we succeed in rising up, we'll only be setting ourselves up for a harder fall back down to where we started. Examples of secondary gains could be our reliance on the security of disability benefits (if we feel ready to try working full time but don't want to risk losing them), telling ourselves that unhealthy relationships are better than being alone (as though we're incapable or unworthy of finding healthier people), or avoiding steps toward recovery out of concern that we'll lose professional supports and services prematurely if we succeed. They're the rationalizations and justifications that only serve to keep us stuck, and they're often driven by fear of failure or fear of success. We immobilize ourselves as a result of "impostor syndrome" (when we irrationally convince ourselves that we're not as capable as we're acting) or because progress invites higher levels of expectation from others that we don't yet feel ready to meet. These fears are biased and largely unfounded. None of them even remotely allows for the possibility of things going well, and all of them assume that a setback can't be effectively worked around and resolved. They amount to our subscribing to failure ahead of time, based on what our struggles have taught us to doubt about ourselves.

Self-sabotage is another common obstacle and generally happens when steps forward in recovery are too big or are happening too quickly. Examples would be relapsing to substance use, ending a healthy relationship simply because the safety of it feels unfamiliar, giving up on a school program instead of asking for help, or accumulating absences in a new job until we're fired. While secondary gains prevent us from starting due to the prediction of failure, self-sabotage is the invocation of failure to flee back to the familiarity of where we started.

The ways to overcome these obstacles involve being honest with ourselves about our readiness for change, addressing our fears, using our supports, and pacing ourselves deliberately based on what we know of our own ambivalence. Our reasons for not moving forward are often distorted and based in misunderstanding, and they tend to underestimate what we're capable of. We succeed by pacing ourselves to the point that we're continually challenged but not overwhelmed. We rise above these obstacles by taking a lesson each time they manage to stop us. Each regression or relapse is a learning experience and teaches us the points of vulnerability in ourselves that allowed it to happen. We can use these insights to strengthen our foundation of recovery and prevent relapse in the future.

The strongest obstacles for many survivors are that they remain in dangerous or abusive situations or continue to use substances to self-medicate. These two particular circumstances bring a variety of additional factors and complications to consider, and they demand a primary focus on establishing safety and long-term sobriety, respectively, in order to be overcome.

28. Does "getting well" from trauma mean learning how to avoid things that remind me of what happened?

It's very typical, when we've been traumatized, to feel intuitively driven to avoid internal reminders of what happened (like thoughts, feelings, body sensations, or memories) and external reminders that are triggering but not inherently dangerous. It's completely reasonable and natural that we would have this response because reminders risk inciting all of the symptoms that we don't want to feel. They intrude on us in the form of disturbing memories, flashbacks, nightmares, and waves of heightened anxiety. It would stand to reason that we'd feel compelled to spare ourselves as much of that suffering as we can.

However, avoidance is also what reinforces and maintains fear and, in turn, what perpetuates symptoms of post-traumatic stress. Getting well from trauma ultimately means allowing the brain to access, process, and integrate what happened, without provoking overwhelm, and to recalibrate us back into a sense of proportionate safety. When we continually follow our instinct to avoid what our brains need to work through, we leave that healing process in a state of arrest. Getting well means taking a measured approach in desensitizing to the safe parts of our lives that we've learned to hide from. If we isolate from relationships or minimize time out in the community, the idea of encountering other people becomes more daunting. When we avoid driving or shopping trips or time alone, we're capitulating to the idea that these experiences are somehow dangerous to us, so they begin to feel more dangerous. If we've needed to take time off from work, on short- or long-term disability, it becomes easier with each passing week to lose resolve and question our chances of being able to work again. And when we use alcohol or other drugs to get away from what we're feeling in our heads and bodies, we do it with full awareness that the pain and the memories will still be there, waiting for our return.

These are stuck points, and living in avoidance is what keeps us stuck. It can be much more tempting to find immediate ways out of our suffering, at cost, than it is to work our way through it. But "out" at the expense of "through" simply doesn't carry us forward in trauma recovery. It may help us feel temporarily safer, but it does not help us get well. We maintain our health and safety by staying away from what's actually dangerous: people or scenarios that would be likely to cause us harm. As much as we seek to escape reminders of trauma that aren't legitimate threats, we concede to the fears that unnecessarily incapacitate us.

It should also be said, and emphasized greatly, that becoming "unstuck" is much easier said than done. It would be logical enough to reason that since avoidance is what perpetuates the effects of trauma, the right thing to do would be to go full-force in the opposite direction and to embrace every healthy change possible. But it would be wrong to assume that it's that simple or to expect the change to be a quick fix. Symptoms of PTSD are sometimes misinterpreted by others as a situation where the survivor is somehow failing to "let go of the past." This is not the case. Symptoms persist because the effects of the past haven't yet let go of the survivor. While the inherent danger of what we avoid may not be real, the fear certainly is, and it can have a long-term paralyzing effect on our functioning. It's true that taking steps forward through the fear is the proper course of action, but that's not the entire solution. Those steps need to be taken at a productive pace. Steps too large will be overwhelming and nonproductive and will discourage us from trying again. Steps too small are better than nothing, but they hold us back from realizing what we're capable of. There are professional supports and approaches that are specifically designed for supporting survivors in this process and maximizing the benefit of the effort with the best pacing possible. Please see the answer to question 32 for more on this subject.

The idea of facing and working through what happened can be frightening, like fixing a faulty alarm with a loud air horn that won't stop going off. As we learn the skills to self-regulate and decrease our anxiety and take calculated steps forward, we learn that we're stronger than any noise that alarm can make. We get well by working through our trauma at our own speed and in a way that works best for us. There are many treatments validated for trauma that can help with this process, several of which are covered in the questions that follow.

29. What common elements exist among trauma treatments?

There are a variety of treatment modalities validated for trauma. There are some that directly target the functioning of the brain (like medication and neurofeedback) and others that employ the function of the mind (like EMDR and trauma-focused cognitive behavioral therapy). There are approaches known distinctly for engaging trauma as it's contained in the body (like somatic experiencing and trauma-informed yoga), and programs that harness the power of human connection as a vehicle for recovery (support groups).

Treatment approaches for trauma have several common elements. The first is that they begin by assessing a survivor's safety at the start of treatment and as needed throughout the treatment process. With every treatment option, a survivor's safety is paramount. They also generally include education about trauma. This is a collaborative measure, as the education process works in both directions. Treatment providers educate survivors and their families by answering important questions and explaining the common but often confusing effects of what trauma does to us. They describe the treatment approaches that they offer, including what to expect from the process, and the potential benefits and risks that should be considered.

Survivors are the experts of themselves, and they educate providers accordingly. While the symptoms of trauma and their effects may be predictable in some ways, survivors are individually unique and are the authorities in how their trauma has impacted them. They have the right to have treatment options explained and to consent to or refuse any given option. Survivors are the ones who ultimately decide how their recovery is defined and what they're willing to do to achieve it. Good treatment works when the effort is a partnership. Establishing the survivor's safety as the top priority in any treatment approach also depends greatly upon this collaboration.

Another aspect that treatment approaches share is the objective to improve symptom management and decrease sympathetic dominance in the survivor's nervous system. This can come from learning and practicing specific skill sets for decreasing anxiety and mitigating distress, improving self-care, and expanding our connection in healthy relationships—each a vital component in developing resilience and self-efficacy.

With the exception of approaches like medication, which are strictly brain-based, trauma treatments typically involve, in some way, putting distress management skills to practice while processing the trauma itself. Processing is a term for "working through" what happened. We access the reactive thoughts, beliefs, and feelings we carry beneath the surface and integrate them into our conscious awareness. We give release to the emotional charge held in our minds and bodies, allowing these wounds a chance to finally heal. Treatment approaches will often emphasize meta-cognition (observing and evaluating our own thought patterns) and/or interoception (mindfully attending to what we feel in our bodies) in different ways and will sometimes involve the creation and expression of a "trauma narrative." A trauma narrative is a structured means of expressing the story of what happened to us. Creating it helps us bring our memories into chronological order, gain insight and modify our related beliefs when necessary, access and discharge the emotions within, and reconsolidate our memories with new perspectives. Treatment is paced in such a way as to allow survivors to confront the effects of their trauma while keeping their stress regulated and maintaining a sense of safety. This generates forward momentum without inducing overwhelm and facilitates a healing process that didn't get a chance to be completed when the trauma was occurring.

Trauma treatment also helps us plan and take the steps to reclaim or design a life outside of what trauma has taken away from us. It helps us problem-solve life stresses and address co-occurring conditions like depression, addiction, or other mental health concerns. We make relapse prevention plans and we chart directions for personal growth, shaped uniquely by our own insights and goals.

Treatment teams often consist of providers among multiple disciplines, combining services like medication management, psychotherapy, case management, and community- or home-based support. Partners, family, and friends can also play pivotal roles in encouraging survivors toward their goals.

Every treatment approach has potential benefits and risks. One of the risks of every treatment is that it may not work. Another is that our stress will likely increase at times before it gets better, even when a treatment is working effectively. Some treatments are more intensive than others, and our safety level, readiness, and capacity for distress tolerance need to be considered before they're implemented. Certain intensive treatment approaches may not be indicated if we're experiencing self-harm, psychosis, or active substance use; have had a recent hospitalization; are at moderate or high risk for suicide; or are showing signs of threat toward others. Sometimes the best and most necessary priority of focus needs to be stabilizing symptoms and ensuring safety before trauma can be treated and processed more directly.

For as many similarities as we can find, there are also profound distinctions between treatment approaches for trauma. While many of them have proven in research and in practice to have remarkable success rates, they're distinguished by vast differences in their methodology. Some are determined to be "evidence-based." This means that they've been evaluated scrupulously with controlled clinical studies and have, to the general satisfaction of researchers and practitioners, been established as models that are consistently and reliably effective. There is no one treatment that successfully resolves trauma for every single person who tries it. People respond differently to different methods, so it's to our benefit that we have the variety in approaches that we do. If one idea doesn't work, it doesn't mean that the others won't. Survivors may also find better results from treatment modalities if they return to them for subsequent attempts at later stages of their recovery. This may be because they have more supports in place than they previously did because they feel more ready for participation in the treatment, or because other mitigating factors have been accounted for. The questions that follow will address several of these approaches as well as some of the distinguishing characteristics between them.

30. What is EMDR?

EMDR stands for eye movement desensitization and reprocessing, a treatment modality that was discovered and developed by psychologist Francine Shapiro, PhD. In the book she coauthored, *EMDR: The Breakthrough Therapy for Overcoming Anxiety, Stress, and Trauma*, Dr. Shapiro and Forrest described her theory that our minds have an innate psychological ability to heal themselves. EMDR is a treatment that helps access and facilitate that intuitive healing process (Shapiro & Forrest, 2004). It's a multifaceted approach in that it engages the brain's own natural means of processing, guided by its own revelations, our cognitive and emotional reactions, and our interoception of where those emotional reactions are held in our bodies. EMDR is distinctive among other treatments in that it sometimes allows us to alleviate the effects of multiple traumas concurrently.

EMDR is unique in its inclusion of "bilateral stimulation." This is the use of visual, tactile, or auditory stimuli perceived in an alternating back-and-forth pattern on opposite sides of the body or field of vision. EMDR got its name because the means of bilateral stimulation originally and most commonly used was horizontal movement of the eyes. When our eyes move repeatedly to the left and right, brain activity is activated in a manner similar to when we're experiencing REM sleep. Bilateral stimulation can also be achieved with audio stimuli (wearing headphones that alternate the sound back and forth) or tactile stimulation (e.g., holding pulsers that vibrate alternately in the hands). When this activation is paired with a focus on internal experiences related to trauma, it appears to mobilize the healing process. The theory of EMDR holds that when trauma is accessed and the brain is activated in this way, the mind is able to finally engage and process the trauma to completion.

Following the intake interview, this approach begins with psychoeducation about trauma and about the treatment itself, and an assessment of the survivor's safety and readiness for it. These are basic components of preparation that are typical among trauma therapies. An assessment is then completed to determine the impact of the targeted traumatic event as it resides in the mind (reactive cognitions), the level of distress associated with it, the survivor's emotional responses, and related body sensations. The EMDR clinician shows the survivor exercises for "resource installation," which help to facilitate connection to inner sources of strength and feelings of safety.

EMDR therapists then guide survivors to place their mental focus on aspects of their memory of the trauma and their internal experiences related to it, and to hold that awareness through "sets" of bilateral stimulation (e.g., eyes following the therapist's finger or another point of focus as it moves back and forth). This is done repeatedly, with an evolving shift of mental focus according to where the brain and body take the process. Resource installation and other exercises for relaxation continue to be used as needed to help contain and mitigate distress. As treatment progresses, the trauma experience is worked through, the mind shifts to more adaptive perspectives, and symptoms are relieved.

There are applications for EMDR in treating other conditions as well, including other manifestations of anxiety, low self-esteem, and problems related to addiction. Psychologists with extensive experience in EMDR have discovered and devised new and complementary techniques with a basis in EMDR theory. David Grand, PhD, for example, found impressive results with an approach he calls "brainspotting," which involves trauma processing with the eyes fixed at particular coordinates as opposed to moving back and forth. Philip Manfield, PhD, discovered a means of using bilateral stimulation to diminish stress related to a traumatic memory without actively thinking about it. He calls this the "flash technique" and currently defines and recommends it as a preparatory measure for more standard EMDR treatment as opposed to a stand-alone treatment approach ("The Flash Technique," n.d.).

When the initial research on EMDR and on its results was first presented to the greater mental health community in the 1980s, it was met with reasonable skepticism because of both the questionable inclusion of bilateral stimulation as a primary component and the surprising success rates that were reported. EMDR has since been substantiated by a great amount of research and has established itself worldwide as a remarkably effective treatment modality. It's identified as a Category A recommended treatment for veterans by U.S. Department of Veterans Affairs, is recognized for its efficacy by the American Psychological Association, and is endorsed by the World Health Organization as a valid treatment for trauma (EMDR Institute, n.d.).

31. What is trauma-focused CBT?

Trauma-focused cognitive behavioral therapy (also referred to as TF-CBT) is a treatment designed to help traumatized children (as young as three years old), adolescents, and older teens. It was developed by Judith Cohen, MD, Esther Deblinger, PhD, and Anthony Mannarino, PhD, and is explained in their book, *Treating Trauma and Traumatic Grief in Children and Adolescents* (Cohen, Mannarino, & Deblinger, 2017). TF-CBT was designed as a conjoint approach that actively involves the child's caregiver as an integral part of the treatment process. If a parent's involvement in the treatment isn't possible or isn't a safe option, this important role can be fulfilled by another supportive and prominent adult in the young person's life.

TF-CBT is similar to other trauma treatments in that it begins with education about the effects of trauma and what to expect from the treatment process, how to ascertain and enhance safety, and how to improve symptom management. Kids learn how to identify and express both simple and more complex emotions. They learn skills for recognizing and decreasing their levels of distress and for achieving relaxation in their bodies. When necessary, safety plans are developed to address behaviors of self-injury or suicidal thoughts. TF-CBT includes a component for assisting caregivers with their parenting skills as well, including how to address and manage behaviors common to trauma and how they can help their children practice the coping skills they're learning in therapy.

Children are taught in an age-appropriate way how to assess their own thinking and to recognize distortions in their worldviews (first with everyday life situations and then later with regard to the trauma itself). This helps them in understanding that fears and assumptions aren't the same as facts and in challenging and modifying patterns of thinking that contribute to anxiety, shame, and fear. TF-CBT also implements in vivo desensitization strategies (see the next question) to help eliminate anxiety from triggers and other effects of trauma.

The processing of the trauma itself comes in the form of a uniquely crafted narrative. One of the strengths of TF-CBT is that it's highly customizable, and this component of the treatment process is a shining example of its versatility. The form of the trauma narrative is limited only by the imagination. TF-CBT therapists help children tell their stories through chapter books, poems, comic strips, or collages of pictures. They're told with the use of puppet shows, drawings, and songs. The ultimate point of the narrative isn't the form that the finished product takes; it's the experience of making it. When children put the story of what happened to them into a narrated timeline with a beginning, middle, and end, their charged fragments of memory come together and take the form of an autobiographical account. Emotions are processed, self-blame and fearful assumptions are challenged and resolved, and symptoms of PTSD diminish.

This treatment culminates with the child presenting and telling the story in a conjoint session with the caregiver. The adult is informed and prepared for this step by the TF-CBT therapist ahead of time. This allows for a higher level of healing exposure. It gives children an opportunity to describe their experiences on their terms and in their own words and to demonstrate the empowerment that they've gained in the treatment process. It allows the caregiver to see how far the child has come and to reinforce that healing by expressing support and praise as the narrative is shared. During the treatment and as the end of it approaches, children are helped to find meaning from their experiences and to acknowledge the strengths they've discovered in themselves.

TF-CBT is backed by a significant amount of research. It's been rated a "Model Program and Best Practice" for abused and traumatized children by SAMHSA's National Child Traumatic Stress Network (NCTSN) ("TF-CBT Training Package," 2019).

32. What is in vivo desensitization?

In vivo desensitization is a means of eliminating phobias and trauma-based anxiety responses to situations that are reasonably safe. It involves a gradual and deliberately paced exposure to the triggering scenario, which allows anxiety to alleviate and the mind to adjust to a recognition of safety. This is a method often utilized in psychotherapy.

The approach begins by creating a scale of expected difficulty for varying levels of exposure, ranging from 0 (no anxiety at all) to 10 (the highest anxiety imaginable). For people with a phobia of driving over bridges, for example, a 10 situation might be slowing the car to a crawl in the middle of one. An expected 0 may be sitting in the car while parked in their driveway. A midpoint scenario is then identified (around a 5 on the scale). One person's 5 may involve parking the car on the side of the road with a bridge in sight in the distance. Another person's 5 might be crossing a bridge as a passenger in the back seat. Someone else may reach a 5 level of anxiety just by sitting at home looking at a picture of a bridge. These midpoint scenarios vary from person to person and represent the ideal range where in vivo desensitization work is to be done.

Participants are shown strategies they can use to bring their anxiety down, and these are practiced in session and as homework. The next step is to put themselves into their 5 scenario for prolonged periods of time and repeatedly (e.g., an hour at a time, three times per week). At a midpoint level of difficulty, this should be expected to be challenging but not by any means overwhelming. As people remain in their 5 situation, their minds register both consciously and subconsciously that they're not actually in danger, and anxiety gradually lessens. While they're welcome and encouraged to use their anxiety management strategies if needed, participants typically find that their anxiety declines on its own. The mind itself recalibrates to a more grounded understanding of its own safety. This process is called "habituation." When we stick it out and, by our own choice, stay in a moderately frightening but safe situation for lengthy periods of time and return to that situation frequently, we become less frightened of it. Just as avoidance of anxiety-provoking situations reinforces fear, controlled and deliberate exposure in the face of that anxiety eliminates it.

Repetition helps progress to take root and maintain. As they keep returning to the same situation, people find that the exposure becomes easier and easier. Their related anxiety begins to elevate to no higher than a 4 and then to no higher than a 3. When the difficulty level with that original scenario diminishes to a 1 or a 0, the question then becomes "What would be around a 5 now?" How has the midpoint evolved? The new 5 might be driving repetitively over a short overpass that doesn't have the appearance of a full bridge. The process is then repeated until the difficulty of the second scenario drops, and then repeated again with the one that comes next. As anxiety lowers and confidence builds, what used to be a 10 eventually falls within the much more achievable range of "challenging but not overwhelming." The same approach is applied once again, and the phobia or trigger response is ultimately extinguished.

These exercises can include support from others. Some people's definition of a 5 may involve placing themselves in a situation with a loved one or professional "coach" (such as a community-based mental health service provider) at their side or close by. As desensitization progresses, their partners gradually distance themselves as part of the process.

In its applications for trauma, the same strategies are used but with exposure to situations that survivors have avoided because of what happened to them. These could be direct reminders of the trauma (like tolerating time in a car following an accident) or common life activities that they've come to evade (like time spent in crowded places like supermarkets or malls). For children, in vivo desensitization can be used to reduce anxiety from experiences like spending time alone or tolerating the dark at bedtime. The process works in much the same way as it does for phobias. It's very effective for countering our drive for avoidance and relieving the anxiety that underlies it.

In vivo desensitization is a method meant for the elimination of disproportionate or irrational anxiety in everyday life situations ("in vivo" means "in life.") It's never to be used in situations that are actually dangerous or harmful. A question that might be asked by a survivor is "I'm triggered by situations all the time. I feel like I'm exposed to them every day. Why isn't my anxiety going down?" The answer lies in the approach. When symptoms are activated continually and unpredictably, anxiety will likely be fluctuating and peaking at points much higher than a 5 on our scales. Triggers don't happen on our terms. A systematic means of approaching them absolutely does. When it's planned and executed carefully, with support, we're in charge of the process. We carefully and gradually confront our trauma-based associations without reaching the point of overwhelm and take more advanced steps in accordance with the strength we accumulate.

In vivo desensitization is often incorporated into trauma treatment and is a featured component of some modalities. It's used prominently in trauma-focused cognitive behavioral therapy (see question 31) and prolonged exposure therapy (question 33) and is otherwise used as a reliable adjunctive strategy in other approaches.

33. What is prolonged exposure therapy?

Just as in vivo desensitization helps with exposure to reminders of trauma (see question 32), the concept behind it has been found to work very effectively with traumatic memories as well. Edna Foa, PhD, theorized this connection and originated one of the first and most effective modern treatments for trauma. She called it "prolonged exposure therapy" (PE) and described how it worked in her coauthored book titled *Reclaiming Your Life from a Traumatic Experience: Workbook* (Rothbaum, Foa, & Hembree, 2007).

This approach begins with education about the effects of trauma and an introduction to the treatment process, as well as establishing safety and teaching survivors how to decrease anxiety when they're feeling activated. A strategy commonly taught in PE therapy is to take a regular breath followed by a long, drawn-out exhale. This can decrease anxiety and bring relaxation to the body when it's done repeatedly and is one of several skills used through the process.

In vivo desensitization is a staple of this modality and is used to defuse anxiety responses to external triggers and their associations. The pacing of this process is customized to the readiness and needs of each person. If an expected difficulty level turns out to be incorrect (too easy or too challenging), the plan is adjusted to account for it. By scoring and tracking their distress as it reduces over time, survivors are rewarded with tangible evidence that they're becoming stronger as their trauma responses fade. Their minds gradually reprogram themselves to encounter these situations without the reactive assumption that they carry a threat. As anxiety diminishes and loses its power, higher levels of exposure become more easily tolerated. Self-efficacy is recognized and strengthened, extending the reach of what's possible in terms of recovery and resilience.

The most defining characteristic of PE therapy is its inclusion of repeated and prolonged imaginal exposure to traumatic memories. When a survivor is able to access these memories with anxiety managed and muscles relaxed (through skills that have been learned and demonstrated), it opens the way for the brain to process what it couldn't process before. In practice, this means that the survivor sits in the therapy session, often with eyes closed, and verbally recalls the trauma, in first person and present tense. As the survivor does this while keeping anxiety regulated, facilitating feeling but preventing overwhelm, the process allows abreaction and healing to take place. Abreaction is access to the emotions that didn't get a chance to be felt and expressed when the trauma happened, allowing for a cathartic release. This is different from emotions or distress felt in a flashback. While flashbacks and trigger reactions don't carry survivors forward in recovery and represent a stuck process, abreaction heals and allows the feelings to become "unstuck" and felt to a point of resolution.

People can sometimes struggle, at first, with telling the story of what happened to them, for several reasons. When we're triggered and our anxiety is overactivated, we lose neocortical function and have difficulty concentrating and putting our experiences into language. The mind's default response to trauma is to avoid upsetting feelings and reminders, so details or whole parts of our traumatic memories may feel lost to us. For these reasons, it's not unusual to begin by reciting our trauma narratives with a relatively brief and spotty account of what happened. Someone who survived a car accident may say, "I remember driving on Main Street and taking a left, getting hit, and then emergency lights, someone holding my hand, and most of my time at the hospital that night." By recalling the memory in narrative form and in present tense, and doing it repeatedly, the story often expands and rounds out. "I see the other car before it crosses the yellow lines." "It's a paramedic holding my hand, but I'm not looking at her. I'm looking up at a police officer who's talking to me." "My mother and brother are at the hospital by my bedside, and we're all talking to the doctor." The puzzle comes together, and as its pieces are picked up and spoken into form, the emotions that charged them are accessed and given a chance to be released. During this process, PE therapists guide survivors to recognize the cognitive distortions that sustained their feelings of fear and self-blame and to adopt new and more accurate perspectives.

PE therapy involves the audio recording of sessions, including one in which anxiety management skills are discussed (a reference for when a refresher is needed) as well as a session in which the narrative is repeatedly told. Survivors listen to the narrative recordings between sessions, and they score and keep track of distress levels before, during, and after each time. Progress is measured in much the same way as it is with in vivo desensitization exercises. Scorecards reflect lower and lower distress ratings as weeks go by and homework is completed.

Prolonged exposure therapy offers a chance to desensitize with exposure to our trauma memories themselves, just as we would desensitize with exposure to external triggering situations. As our reactive beliefs and emotions are accessed and sufficiently worked through, symptoms of PTSD are alleviated.

34. What is internal family systems therapy?

Internal family systems (IFS) therapy originated from the work of psychologist Richard Schwartz, PhD, and is explained and detailed in his coauthored book, *Internal Family Systems Therapy* (Schwartz & Sweezy, 2020). It's predicated on the beautiful theory that while trauma may injure us, all of our mind's reactions are intended in their own way to be helpful and to serve a protective purpose. This modality theorizes that we're all equipped with a core self, an absolute center of identity that existed prior to trauma, persisted through the results of trauma, and continues to exist to this day. This core self simply cannot be damaged, regardless of what's happened in life, but it does become distanced from our conscious awareness. That distance is filled with the inner pains we carry as well as the defenses launched by protective parts of ourselves that are trying their best to ensure our survival.

This treatment involves a considerable amount of mindful introspection, following clues from what we experience in our minds and bodies. Our thoughts and feelings are regarded as "trailheads" that, when recognized and followed, lead to important discoveries about the suffering we've endured and how our minds have adjusted to cope with it. The approach also embraces interoception, as awareness of our body sensations can reveal troves of information about our emotional pain and the messages that lie therein. With guidance from an IFS-trained therapist, we become more cognizant of our protective parts. Insights come forward, and our inner defenses, which have a functional intention even when their methods appear self-destructive, reveal their purposes. In the course of IFS treatment, a survivor may say something like, "I think this part of me that constantly tells myself I'm stupid and useless is happening because it feels safer than the alternative. It's protecting me from something worse. If I'm cruel to myself and kick myself when I'm down, I can't fall any farther than I already am, right? If I admit that I actually don't deserve it, and that I never did, I don't know how I'd handle that. I'd have to accept that life really was that unfair and that people who were supposed to love me really were that terrible. The idea that I deserved love and was still hurt this badly . . . that feels like it would be too much for me to bear right now."

As our protective parts agree to "relax" and reveal their function, they give way to the underlying emotional pain that they've been working to contain. This introspection is a paced and carefully directed process, working from the outside in and lifting layer after layer of emotional injuries and their protective mechanisms. As these layers are accessed and worked through, we eventually uncover the most vulnerable and injured parts of ourselves. Like other trauma treatments, IFS therapy allows us to connect with the suffering that wasn't allowed to be processed when it happened, and to finally feel and cathartically express what had previously gone unspoken. We gain clarity and insight about the facets of ourselves that work to prevent our pain, those that seek to stop the pain at all costs, and those that are left to carry the worst of our suffering beneath the surface. As we heal, these parts of ourselves will continue to exist and serve in their respective functions, but they will adopt healthier and more adaptive ways to do so.

In a process referred to as "unblending," IFS shows us when we've overidentified with characteristics of our protective parts and mistaken pieces as a representation of the whole. It can be very difficult to let go of excessive guilt—to cite one example—if we believe that the desperate choices we made in times of crisis define the entirety of who we are. As we gain perspective of the full picture, we learn to regard these parts of ourselves with compassion and understanding. When this treatment process reaches a particular threshold of depth, beneath the pockets of pain and the parts that took on their protective roles, we become reacquainted with the actual center of who we are. This core self exists and thrives regardless of anything that's happened to us and in spite of what we've done to survive it. It's a self that is unbroken, joyful, peaceful, compassionate, and curious. This is arguably a return to our "original settings" as human beings, which brings benefit beyond the healing of trauma-based emotional wounds. We cope much more effectively with future adversity when we're connected and online with our core selves because they represent the truest source of practically every internal asset related to the development of resilience.

35. Can hypnosis be used for trauma treatment?

Hypnosis was a frontline and commonly practiced treatment option for trauma and anxiety, along with psychoanalysis, from the late 1800s through much of the twentieth century. It was widely used in the field of mental health and sometimes applied in general health care as well. Hypnosis continues to be used today but does not enjoy the same breadth of acceptance and popularity in the professional field of trauma therapy that it did in the past. It does certainly have continued utility and potential, and there's question as to whether and how it may return as a mainstream practice.

The theory behind hypnosis is that we have a conscious mind, by which we aim our focus and perceive what we're noticing and experiencing, and an underlying subconscious, which is always active and working in the background. The subconscious contains and governs the majority of the processes behind the vast and intricate network of memories, beliefs, values, drives, and habits that create the context of our mental space. Hypnosis is a process by which our conscious mind is induced to profound rest while the subconscious remains attentive and emerges to a more surface level. This process brings us into a trance state, which can be achieved to varying degrees of depth. A deeper experience of trance is referred to as "somnambulism." When a trance state is achieved, it can be used as a forum for our memories to be accessed and for our related beliefs and drives to be consulted and modified. The theory of hypnosis is that this enhances the mind's capacity to consider and incorporate new information, as it's guided to new and more adaptive shifts in perspective.

In its application for trauma treatment, hypnosis begins with a safety screening and assessment, education about trauma, and an introduction to the process of hypnosis and how it works. A question commonly asked by people seeking hypnosis is "Can I be hypnotized?" Trance is a state of mind that we've all experienced at least to a mild extent. If you've ever driven on a highway and realized you've passed several exits without realizing it, or found yourself daydreaming to the point that you lost track of what was being said to you, you've experienced a light version of the trance phenomenon. Generally speaking, this state can be accessed and deepened as long as you can relax and follow instructions. Hypnosis treatment of any kind is arguably more of a guided self-hypnosis exercise than anything else because it relies upon a person's cooperation in following the instructions for induction and treatment.

Methods used in hypnosis for trauma can be direct or indirect in their application. They may involve a return to traumatic memories, accessed and observed from a place of relaxation. As with other treatments, this revisiting of the memory allows for cathartic abreaction, processing and integration of what happened, and recognition of more resilient insights. As with internal family systems therapy (see question 34), some methods of hypnosis involve consulting with different parts of ourselves when they're conflicted in their protective reactions. Other methods in hypnosis don't broach the trauma directly but appeal to the subconscious healing process through hypnotic metaphor (relating generally to adversity and how we can cope better with it) and a process of cognitive restructuring (challenging and modifying beliefs that perpetuate avoidance or fear).

As with any kind of therapy, hypnosis isn't a panacea and isn't necessarily the best or most effective solution for some survivors. Hypnosis also is not as regulated as other practices. States may differ in their standards for what's allowed, but, by and large, a hypnosis practitioner doesn't necessarily need to be a licensed health care professional or have any accredited degree related to the study of mental health. When seeking hypnosis treatment, survivors can inform their search by asking for the qualifications of practitioners, including the licenses or certifications they hold, the extent of their expertise with hypnosis, and their training and experience in its applications for trauma.

36. What is neurofeedback?

Neurofeedback, like medication, is a means of directly affecting change in the brain itself. The brain's functioning depends on activity and communication between neurons, which happen in two ways: chemically, through neurotransmitters; and electrically, through brain waves. Both of these mechanisms can be targeted and adjusted with treatment. Our culture in the United States has embraced a preference for chemical intervention, in the form of psychotropic medication. But there's also been significant effort in research worldwide to develop our understanding of brain wave patterns as they're associated with psychiatric symptoms, and how this insight can be applied in treatment for trauma and other conditions.

Neurofeedback is a remarkable application of operant conditioning in that it modifies brain wave activity by rewarding the brain itself with positive reinforcement. In other words, with the use of EEG technology, this approach encourages the brain to shift its electrical impulses in a desired direction and to do so repeatedly until those changes take hold and become the norm. As those shifts become habitual, brain function improves and symptoms decrease.

After an initial assessment and introduction to neurofeedback, the treatment typically begins with a process of "brain mapping." A cap with sensors is placed over the participant's head, and a reading of brain wave activity is taken. Neurofeedback software translates this data to show where activity in different parts of the brain is higher or lower than a common baseline (i.e., the typical levels that you'd see from someone who doesn't have trauma symptoms).

Once that process is done, a series of sessions are planned for the operant training itself. Participants have sensors placed on those areas of the head where the targeted brain waves are happening, and then they sit or lie down comfortably. They're then given access to a movie, video game, or other sensory stimulus and watch the screen. As those targeted brain waves shift more toward the desired frequency, the brain is rewarded in the context of the stimuli. If our neurofeedback tool involves watching a movie, the film we're watching will go out of focus and darken when our brain wave signals shift in the wrong direction. When our activity veers toward the desired state, the movie will brighten and come back into clarity. If the tool is a video game, the more our brain waves improve, the more our video game character moves toward its objective. When our readings don't go in the right direction, the character stays put. The brain does the work on its own and begins to favor the new patterns. While this requires no conscious effort on the part of the survivor, treatment sessions can feel mentally exhausting. When done regularly and for a long enough period of time, these changes reach a threshold by which the new activity pattern consolidates and maintains itself.

The website for the Trauma Center at the Justice Resource Institute describes studies conducted there on the efficacy of neurofeedback in helping traumatized children and adults. Their outcomes found neurofeedback to bring "highly significant improvement" to executive functioning ("Neurofeedback," n.d.). Executive functioning includes our capacity to focus, to react without impulsivity, and to create new solutions to problems. This suggests that neurofeedback could help survivors not only alleviate certain symptoms of PTSD but also gain a concurrent rise in overall cognitive resilience.

Neurofeedback holds promise as an effective treatment for trauma. Because it harnesses a focus on electrophysiology instead of pharmacology, it's not as popular or available in the United States as it is in other parts of the world. As more research is done in our country, and as the practice of it becomes more mainstream, its value as a standard trauma treatment may become more widely recognized.

37. What are somatic experiencing and sensorimotor therapies?

The untold story of our suffering finds its home in the body as much as in the mind, held and expressed through the physical sensations of shame, anger, fear, and sadness. In the moments when we first encounter overwhelming trauma and our fight, flight, or freeze response is activated (see question 6), our bodies correspond with instinctive movements geared toward defense (e.g., hitting or pushing away), escape (running), or constriction (making ourselves small and hiding). Our bodies hold an implicit retention of energy from these reactions, wired and encoded through our nerve networks. This stored charge expresses through habitual muscle tension, reflexive movements, protective postures, and changes in how we breathe. An anxiety-ridden body also compromises our neocortical functioning, impairing our ability to focus and to tolerate the stresses and emotions that we feel. This creates a reciprocated cycle of activation. There are specialized therapies that developed out of this understanding and were shown to be very effective in helping survivors toward recovery.

Somatic experiencing (SE) originated from the work of Peter A. Levine, PhD. In his book *Waking the Tiger: Healing Trauma*, Levine described the fight, flight, or freeze reactions as constituting a "unified defense system." He explained that when fight or flight aren't possible, the body will react to that helplessness by turning to its freeze response as its last resort. This constricts the energy that would have been expended by fighting or running, and binds the nervous system into a state of fear-charged immobilization. The sensations involved with finally coming out of that immobility response feel chaotic and dangerous. Our avoidance of these feelings creates a perpetuated pattern of containment, so the inner sense of helplessness becomes indefinitely sustained (1997, pp. 99–101). Levine realized that to resolve trauma, in a process he calls "renegotiation," its discharge needs to be facilitated in a manner that allows for completion of the instinctive response and a resolution of what drives it (Levine, 1997, p. 179).

Through SE, these trapped reactive responses are gently encountered and given a means of release. Using gestures, postures, exercises, and breath work, SE therapists introduce survivors to tools for self-regulation and decreasing distress. This treatment invites the body to kinetically express and complete the defensive responses it's retained and to discharge its underlying traumatic energy. Unlike more cognitive-based therapies, SE doesn't prioritize a verbal narrative so much as it invites the body to react and communicate on its own terms, and it's been shown in research to bring impressive results in doing so (Brom et al., 2017). In their article titled "Somatic Experiencing: Using Interoception and Proprioception as Core Elements of Therapy," Payne, Levine, and Crane-Godreau described three focal components to this modality: resourcing, titration, and pendulation. "Resourcing" introduces survivors to inner feelings of relaxation and confidence. "Titration" is described as a gentle approach to the "edge" of the activation caused by the trauma, at a level that's manageable and not overwhelming. "Pendulation" is the practice of alternating back and forth between titration and resourcing, which allows for a gradual progression of processing and kinesthetic release. This helps survivors access their trauma activation bit by bit, discharge its energy while remaining regulated, and gain increased tolerance and resilience as they go (Payne, Levine, & Crane-Godreau, 2015).

Sensorimotor psychotherapy was developed in collaboration between Pat Ogden, PhD, and Kekuni Minton, PhD. It shares several qualities with SE in theory and practice but has some differing characteristics as well. Dr. Ogden remarked on this comparison in her article, "Sensorimotor Psychotherapy: One Method for Processing Traumatic Memory." She acknowledged that both approaches track physical sensations and find somatic means of bringing suffocated reactive physical gestures to completion. This helps survivors explore and work their way out of conditioned body responses that perpetuate helplessness and hold them back in recovery. She explained that what makes sensorimotor psychotherapy stand out is that it ultimately carries the process into a more explicit and holistic combination of sensorimotor, cognitive, and emotional processing (Ogden & Minton, 2000). A more regulated body brings greater neocortical functioning and improved concentration. Dr. Ogden's method takes advantage of these benefits by working through the thoughts, beliefs, and feelings that sustain a reciprocal relationship with our trauma-based body sensations. She believes that this comprehensive approach helps maximize the potential of the treatment.

In their book, *Sensorimotor Psychotherapy: Interventions for Trauma and Attachment*, Dr. Ogden and Janina Fisher, PhD, described three phases of this treatment. In the first phase, they begin by helping survivors improve confidence and learn skills for self-regulation. The second phase involves focusing on memories and their lasting and sometimes implicit effects, recognizing and reorganizing how trauma is held in the body, and processing related thoughts and emotions. The third phase, which they call "Moving Forward," helps survivors with finding meaning, challenging limiting beliefs, setting goals, and making the changes necessary to achieve more satisfaction in life (Ogden & Fisher, 2016).

Body-oriented therapies take a unique approach to the treatment of trauma. As we attune to the feelings and messages we hold somatically and allow ourselves to work through the expression of these sensations, our long-held charge of fear finally finds release. Trauma is processed in both body and mind, awarding survivors with relief from symptoms and an overall improvement in physiological resilience.

38. What medications are prescribed in the treatment of trauma?

The only two medications currently approved by the U.S. Food and Drug Administration for treatment of PTSD are both selective serotonin reuptake inhibitors. One is called sertraline (the generic name for Zoloft), and the other is paroxetine (the generic name for Paxil) (Alexander, 2012). These same medications are recommended by The National Center for PTSD at the U.S. Department of Veterans Affairs for treatment of traumatized veterans, along with two others, fluoxetine (Prozac) and venlafaxine (Effexor), which have been found in studies to be effective for treating trauma (National Center for PTSD, n.d.-a).

Other types of medications used frequently in the treatment of PTSD are prescribed "off-label." Blood pressure medications like Clonidine and Prazosin have been found to be effective for some survivors in alleviating nightmares. Clonidine is also known to reduce flashbacks and to help diminish reactive anxiety. Atypical antipsychotic medications like Seroquel or Risperdal can be helpful with short-term use, as these medications are calming, allow for improved sleep, and in larger doses can help stabilize mood. Side effects need to be taken carefully into account. Antipsychotics, for example, have metabolic contraindications to consider, including weight gain and adverse effects on blood sugar.

Medications for trauma are commonly prescribed in combination with one another. A full treatment regimen for a PTSD survivor may begin with a recommended antidepressant like Zoloft, which may prove helpful but can take weeks to work. An antipsychotic medication like Risperdal or a benzodiazepine like Ativan or Klonopin may be prescribed to alleviate distress and improve sleep in the meantime, until the antidepressant takes effect. While benzodiazepines can be helpful for many survivors in the short term, they've been known to bring additional challenges as well. When used for a lengthy period of time, especially with relatively high doses, tapering off them can be a long and arduous process. The VA National Center for PTSD recommends against the use of benzodiazepines for PTSD, stating simply on its website that "there are better treatment options" (National Center for PTSD, n.d.-b). The Center acknowledges the utility of benzodiazepines in short-term applications but warns that they can bring some significant and adverse long-term effects, as survivors may become dependent. It also cautions that when survivors rely upon benzodiazepines to escape reminders of trauma, it inhibits them from learning how to otherwise cope with their symptoms. This arguably sustains the cycle of avoidance, making it harder in the long term to recover from PTSD.

The U.S. military has been researching an innovative new treatment for PTSD symptoms, and the results so far have been very promising. In June 2019, *60 Minutes*, on CBS, reported that the U.S. Army was spending $2,000,000 to investigate a procedure called "stellate ganglion block," or "SGB." The report described SGB as a local anesthetic that's injected into a nerve cluster, called the "stellate ganglion," that helps control the brain's fight or flight reactions. The treatment was found to decrease the severity of PTSD symptoms, and while the medication cleared the body within a day, the effects were found to last up to six months or longer (Whitaker, 2019). In November 2019, CBS provided an update, reporting that the Army-funded trial found SGB treatment to reduce symptoms of PTSD at about twice the rate of the placebo (Abbot & Polevoy, 2019).

Psychotherapy is often recommended in tandem with medication, as the combined approach is found to enhance treatment outcomes. Prescribers will sometimes offer therapy services themselves but frequently work in collaboration with other providers.

39. How can massage, yoga, acupuncture, and acupressure help trauma survivors?

Trauma interrupts our ability to perceive the emotions and stress harbored in our bodies by dissociating those feelings from our conscious awareness. When we feel safe enough to explore our inner physical sensations with curiosity, on our own terms, our capacity for that connection can be revived and reclaimed. Massage, yoga, acupuncture, and acupressure all offer opportunities to alleviate somatic and emotional distress and facilitate a gradual reconciliation with the feelings our bodies hold.

Massage therapists are very familiar with this process. They recognize how easily stress translates into muscle tension and witness the profound emotional release that can result when it relaxes. Massage will sometimes bring people to tears when certain muscle groups finally let go of what they've been carrying. A discharge of muscle tension and emotion together can sometimes be accompanied by unexpected thoughts or memories, revealing important clues to their sources.

Yoga brings similar benefits and is sometimes recommended in trauma therapy as an adjunctive intervention because of its effectiveness in restoring the mind-body connection. Survivors learn to experiment, at a rate of progress within their range of tolerance, with accessing and noticing the feelings that emerge with different poses. They discover how their sensations rise and fall, shifting and transforming with the passing of time, and gradually gain practice in mindfully relaxing into those sensations. Studies have shown that as survivors learn to tolerate sensory experiences that were once associated with fear and helplessness, they notice improvement in symptom management and develop gains in resilience (van der Kolk et al., 2014). This can be a difficult and sometimes triggering process, so a careful and deliberate approach is extremely important. There are specialized yoga programs, identified as "trauma-sensitive," which are designed to show survivors how to practice yoga at a pace that's helpful and productive. The Trauma Center at the Justice Resource Institute in Brookline, Massachusetts, developed a trauma-sensitive yoga program that was found to be very effective in reducing the severity of PTSD symptoms and dissociative episodes (Clark et al., 2014). Associates at the Trauma Center announced on their website that in 2017, theirs was the first trauma-sensitive yoga program to be listed as evidence-based in the treatment of psychological trauma (Trauma Center, n.d.).

Some survivors find periods of relief from the use of acupuncture, a Chinese practice that is thousands of years old. Joseph M. Helms, MD, author of *Acupuncture Energetics: A Clinical Approach for Physicians* (1995), explains that the theory of acupuncture involves "qi," a life energy that travels through meridians mapped across the body. Through the insertion of needles in various combinations and patterns into the body, this practice is believed to encourage the improved "flow" of this energy (Helms, 1998). A systematic review of research into the efficacy of acupuncture for trauma found some promising outcomes with regard to its application for reducing anxiety, depressed mood, sleep disturbance, and chronic pain. The researchers noted, however, that the articles reviewed didn't address its application for the entire "trauma spectrum response," including its value in alleviating fatigue or improving cognitive functioning. They called for more research to determine acupuncture's efficacy across a more comprehensive scope of treatment for trauma symptoms (Lee et al., 2012). A separate review declared the effectiveness of acupuncture for PTSD to be "encouraging but not cogent" and also concluded that more trials are needed (Kim et al., 2013).

Acupressure follows the same energy meridian theory as acupuncture, but it uses physical pressure or "tapping" in lieu of needles. A treatment protocol called "emotional freedom technique" (EFT) was developed by Gary Craig in 1995. He explains on the website for his official training centers that EFT "integrates the Chinese meridian system into the therapy process by tapping on meridian points with your fingertips" (Craig, n.d.) EFT is a unique intervention in that it typically involves tapping on these points on the body while focusing on targeted thoughts, beliefs, and images, with the aim of relieving distress specifically related to their content. It has applications for trauma as well, as survivors will talk through their experiences with a trained EFT coach while using the tapping protocol at the most difficult points, neutralizing their anxiety each time it arises. Researchers have found EFT to bring positive outcomes in treatment of PTSD, stating that more than 40 peer-reviewed concept papers and systematic reviews have established it as an evidence-based treatment. They've also noted that because extensive research has shown positive outcomes and no "adverse events," the U.S. Department of Veterans Affairs designated EFT as a "generally safe" therapy for veterans (Church et al., 2018).

By accessing or strengthening our mind-body connection, we gain the ability to tend to emotions and stress that would otherwise be hidden from our conscious awareness. Ongoing research is helping expand our understanding of each of these approaches as well as their value and potential for facilitating recovery in trauma survivors.

40. How can support groups and community groups help in the treatment of trauma?

Community groups, like church congregations, sports teams, exercise or yoga classes, volunteer organizations, clubs, and community theater can all be excellent opportunities to cultivate social connection. They provide a means to decrease isolation, to be part of something outside of ourselves, and to challenge our doubts and fears about being counted and included among others. Healthy relationships are a basic and necessary human need and an integral component to trauma recovery. When we're brave enough to leave our homes and band together toward common interests and goals, we're granted opportunities for finding new friends and developing a sense of fellowship. Some community groups are specifically designed to promote mental health. The National Alliance on Mental Illness (https://nami.org) regularly provides a variety of classes and meetings for those seeking recovery from psychiatric disorders, as well as for their loved ones.

Support groups bring some unique rewards in terms of shared experience and relatability. It can become much easier to find our voices and communicate with other people when we're confident they'll have some personal understanding of what we're saying. This is true for 12-step programs, which can help greatly when we're affected by others' addiction (like Al Anon or Narc Anon), or living with addiction ourselves (e.g., Alcoholics Anonymous, Narcotics Anonymous, Gamblers Anonymous, Sex and Love Addicts Anonymous, Overeaters Anonymous). Support groups allow us to practice trusting again, and to build our confidence about letting our walls down and opening lines of communication. Once we've proven to ourselves that we can do it—and that we can do it repeatedly—showing that same vulnerability to the trusted people in our private lives may become easier.

Trauma-specific groups offer a useful forum for challenging our fears about the world and our insecurities about ourselves. Survivors very often carry the burden of undeserved shame. For as long as we hold these feelings in secret, we deprive ourselves of the opportunity to challenge and resolve them. Social attunement (our ability to empathize and connect with one another) with other survivors gives us a chance to rediscover the beauty, innocence, and potential of the human spirit. When we recognize those values in people we relate to, we can allow for the reality that they also exist in us.

Trauma support groups typically come in one of three types. The first is "peer support," which is a simple forum for survivors to meet one another, discuss common struggles, and share helpful resources and coping strategies. This type of group can be a helpful adjunct to mental health services but doesn't have the same structured direction and therapeutic focus of the other two. The second is called "psychoeducational," which means that the purpose of the group is to learn about PTSD and skills for improving self-care and symptom management. Because their primary purpose is education, these groups will sometimes have structured rules limiting what's shared between members with regard to their personal histories. They add this safeguard to minimize the chance of becoming unexpectedly triggered by details of each other's trauma. The third type is a "processing group," where traumatic experiences are openly talked about and worked through and where participants share in the healing and recovery process. One example of this would be a cognitive processing therapy (CPT) group, a 12-week treatment often recommended for veterans (National Center for PTSD, n.d.).

Support groups are an accessible means of establishing social connection with people who can relate in many ways to the challenges we've faced. They inform our recovery while awarding us the privilege of encouraging the recovery of others. There's a great amount of meaning and benefit to be found when survivors come together, especially when there's a reciprocal exchange of compassion and vulnerability. We have a much easier time dismantling our own rationalizations for self-blame when we hear them reflected and refuted by others who know exactly what we're talking about. As we witness the value and innocence of people who have been injured in similar ways, who react with similar or identical fears and concerns, we can find our own value and innocence reflected back to us.

41. What part does family and social support play in recovery?

Mental health services, like psychotherapy or case management, begin with an "intake assessment." This is an interview that informs service providers about the reasons we're seeking treatment, the strengths and resources we have to draw from, and our relevant life histories, among other things. A question commonly asked in this assessment is "How many people in your life can you count on if you need help?" Equally important questions are "How many relationships in your life do you consider to be healthy?" and "How much contact do you have with them?"

Good social connection fortifies us in recovery from trauma. It is through the bonds of secure relationships that we practice being safe with others. When we have people in our lives who have earned our trust and proven themselves to deserve it, we're rewarded on multiple levels. Loving family and friends can observe and attest to our strengths when we struggle to see them ourselves. When we're feeling discouraged and hopeless, they'll hold onto hope for us until we're able to pick it back up again. We become vitalized when we know that we're not facing our struggles alone. We learn more about who we are and become more acquainted with the truth of our own worth. Social support offers the assurances of a safety net that will catch us when we need it and equips us with a protective boost in resilience when we're faced with adversity in the future.

Loved ones can be valuable allies in trauma treatment, when we choose to include them. They inform mental health service providers with their perspectives, prompt us to use the coping strategies that we've learned, and help in recognizing signs of progress or the lack thereof. Sometimes those people closest to us are the first to notice the earliest warning signs of trouble and can also be the first to recognize a reduction in the severity of our symptoms.

If our families, friends, or partners aren't supportive, are abusive, or otherwise increase our vulnerability to relapse, we have no obligation to involve their participation in any aspect of our treatment or recovery process. The roles that destructive relationships play in our recovery are best defined by the boundaries and distance that we introduce to them.

When we know that we reside in the hearts and minds of others, and that we're seen and heard and cared for, the destructive fears and beliefs in our minds have a longer distance to travel before they reach our hearts. We become armed with confirmation of our value. Our moods become more stable. We become more confident. Goals that once seemed daunting and distant are much more likely to feel within reach when we know we're not facing that journey alone. There are significant benefits to our physical health as well. Just as trauma has been shown to contribute to systemic inflammation and increased rates of disease (see question 10), social support has been found to bring an opposite effect. Emma Seppala, PhD, the science director of Stanford University's Center for Compassion and Altruism Research and Education, has extensively studied and researched the benefits of social connection. In her online article titled "Connectedness & Health: The Science of Social Connection," she notes that people who feel connected to others not only have lower levels of anxiety and depression but also have strengthened immune systems, a higher rate of disease recovery, and a 50 percent increased chance of overall longevity (Seppala, 2014).

Sound relationships are perhaps unequaled in their overall value for improving resilience in trauma survivors. As human beings, we're not meant to be solitary creatures. We're not wired to thrive when we're alone. If we ask ourselves how many healthy supports we have in our lives, and the answer is "zero," this is a call to prioritize finding them (see question 40). To call the effort worthwhile would be an understatement. To call ourselves worthwhile would be a nice first step.

42. What can I do to help a friend or family member suffering from trauma, and who can I contact for help?

When someone we love has been through something terrible, we can easily find ourselves struggling to find "the right things to say." Is it better to talk about what happened or avoid the subject? Are we pushing them too hard or not encouraging them enough? What are the best ways to show we care when times are especially hard? The good news is that we don't need to have all the answers. Perhaps more important than any words we can offer is the gift of our willingness to listen. A survivor will sometimes notice close friends and family behaving differently or distancing themselves after the traumatic event—not because they don't care but because they care greatly and don't know what to say or do. To err on the side of caution, they'll resort to assumptions of what their loved one wants and needs. There's really no need to rely upon assumptions because every question we have can be answered with good communication.

Social connection improves the prognosis for treatment and recovery. It's an engine for developing resilience, and we offer it through our presence, empathy, and compassion. When people are suffering and confused by their symptoms, there's no substitute for a friend or family member who is willing to help. The best way to know how to be there for survivors is to ask the survivors. Let them know that you're available, and ask how you can best support them. Listen attentively. Reflect and validate what you're told. If they don't yet know what kind of support they need, which is entirely possible, make it clear that you're there for them when they do—and in the meantime, as they figure it out.

Respect the boundaries that your loved one sets. Ask about them. Some people benefit from increased attention, assurance, hugs, and the like because being treated differently feels isolating and reinforces trauma-based beliefs (e.g., that they're not lovable, that they're to blame for what happened, or that they're unattractive or scary to others because of it). In those situations, the best thing you can do is keep familiarity in the routine and consistency in the time you spend together. Other survivors need space and may feel triggered or distressed by feeling observed or being touched. They might not be able to participate in activities like they used to and may, instead, need more quiet and alone time than they did in the past. This may shift over time, in either direction, depending on where survivors are in recovery, the impact of their symptoms any given day, and their own changing preferences and needs. Which of these approaches is best for your loved ones? Ask them. There's no need for guesswork about this.

You can also help by respecting survivors' privacy, by the parameters they request. Be mindful of who they want informed about what happened and any limitations they place on that information being shared or spread. It can be easy for survivors to feel overexposed very quickly when information spreads without their permission.

When we educate ourselves about the symptoms of PTSD, a lot of the changes that we see in our loved ones (e.g., irritability, isolation, avoidance) will make sense in context. There are online and community resources that can help. The National Alliance on Mental Illness (https://nami.org) provides classes and support groups for people living with psychiatric disorders as well as for friends and families. It also offers a series of classes through a program called "NAMI Homefront" (NAMI, n.d.), which helps loved ones of military service members better understand the effects of trauma and connects them with services for support.

Encourage your loved one to seek answers to questions as well. Share what you've learned about the common effects of trauma and the treatments that are validated for it. Recovery feels more possible when we know there's help. Referrals to specialized providers can be made by a primary care physician or another health-care professional, or we can do our own research and contact them ourselves. There are online directories available to help you find therapists trained in several of the modalities covered in this section (see them listed in the "Directory of Resources"). It's completely acceptable to call providers and ask about their specializations, experience, and qualifications before scheduling an intake. Your loved one may want your help with this process.

If needed, consider making a plan with the survivor about what you and other supports can do to help in times of crisis. This doesn't mean that you're expected to offer support you don't feel qualified to provide or that you should handle situations alone when they require professional intervention. Offer the assistance that's appropriate to the scope of your relationship. Be aware of emergency support resources in your area that you can reach out to (e.g., 9-1-1, local suicide and crisis hotlines), and use them if necessary. The National Suicide Prevention Hotline can be reached at 1-800-273-8255 (National Suicide Prevention Lifeline, n.d.).

Finally, and equally important to any other point made here, tend to your own self-care. Witnessing the suffering of a loved one can be very distressing, to say the least. Talk to your own supports. Be mindful of your own needs and limits. Get your own professional help if you need it. Tend to your sleep, your eating, your hydration, and your time with friends.

You can't pour from an empty cup. Remember that the best supports for trauma survivors are the people who are healthy themselves. Investing in your own self-care is one of the most important and necessary investments you can make as a support to the person you love.

43. What kinds of treatments help with borderline personality disorder?

Three treatments that have been shown to be effective in the treatment of borderline personality disorder (BPD) are dialectical behavior therapy, mentalization therapy, and schema therapy.

Dialectical behavior therapy (DBT) is a comprehensive treatment approach that was developed by Marsha Linehan, PhD, in the late 1980s. She described her insights and methods in her pioneering books on the subject, *Cognitive Behavioral Treatment of Borderline Personality Disorder* (1993) and the *Skills Training Manual for Treating Borderline Personality Disorder* (2015). Dialectical behavior therapy commonly includes individual therapy and coaching as well as psychoeducational group therapy, which teaches key concepts and skills across four domains: core mindfulness skills, interpersonal effectiveness, distress tolerance, and emotion regulation. The core mindfulness skills are its most foundational component, as they introduce strategies for achieving and holding mental awareness and observing external and internal stimuli from that presence. People with BPD are introduced to the concept of achieving what Linehan referred to as "radical acceptance" of their circumstances while acknowledging their capability and potential for positive change. Linehan also explained that we maximize our efficacy when we validate our emotional responses as much as our ability to think rationally, a concept she referred to as "wise mind."

Dialectical behavior therapy teaches a multitude of skills and strategies for each of the domains. It helps survivors identify and skillfully express emotions, regulate distress and improve symptom management, understand interpersonal boundaries, and get social needs met in their relationships. Skills are practiced and their results recorded with "diary cards," and times of relapse are carefully investigated and reviewed as learning experiences. The skills and concepts of DBT can be easily generalized and helpful to anyone who suffers from emotional distress, so they're often used in therapy treatment of other mental health conditions.

Mentalization therapy is another treatment that involves both individual and group therapy interventions. It was developed and introduced by

Peter Fonagy, PhD, and Anthony Bateman, MD, and explained in their book *Mentalization-Based Treatment for Personality Disorders* (Bateman & Fonagy, 2016). In their journal article titled "Mentalization-Based Treatment for Borderline Personality Disorder," Fonagy and Bateman defined mentalization as "the process by which we make sense of each other and ourselves, implicitly and explicitly, in terms of subjective states and mental processes." They explained that when people with BPD experience emotional distress, particularly in the context of fearing losses in relationships, their capacity for mentalization is diminished. This results in increased emotional sensitivity and impulsive responses, which underlie common symptoms of BPD (Bateman & Fonagy, 2010).

Mentalization therapy draws from relational experiences that survivors have with other people in their lives, but Fonagy and Bateman have written that the relationship between the person with BPD and the therapist is also an important means for validating and exploring these experiences. The two work together to interpret them and collaborate in exploring new perspectives. As with DBT, this process of adopting new ways of thinking introduces more flexibility beyond the polarized, reactive thought process that a distressed mind will gravitate to by default. Survivors improve their mentalization skills by recognizing how their perception of self compares and contrasts with their perceptions of others (Bateman & Fonagy, 2013). This translates to more effective emotion regulation and healthier bonds in relationships and is believed by researchers to decrease impulsivity and suicidal ideation as well (Juul et al., 2019).

Schema therapy was designed by psychologist Jeffrey Young, PhD, and described in his book *Schema Therapy: A Practitioner's Guide* (Young, Klosko, & Weishaar, 2003). In "Schema Therapy for Borderline Personality Disorder," article coauthors Young and Kellogg defined schemas as "deeply entrenched, dysfunctional belief systems," explaining that schema therapy utilizes the therapeutic relationship as a means to model and redefine healthy boundaries and interaction by creating an atmosphere of "safety, stability, and acceptance." The therapy itself involves emotion-focused experiential strategies in session, help with thought assessment and restructuring, and skill building in improving interpersonal interaction and managing anger and distress (Kellogg & Young, 2006).

While both DBT and mentalization therapy involve both group and individual therapy, the typical format for schema therapy includes individual therapy twice a week. Progress is made as survivors apply their insight and develop lasting changes in their patterns of thoughts, beliefs, and choices (Choi-Kain, Finch, Masland, Jenkins, & Unruh, 2017).

Each of these treatments have been shown in research and practice to have great value in helping people living with BPD. They help us rise out of the patterns of black-and-white thinking that are common to complex trauma and cultivate resilience by managing symptoms objectively and with insight.

44. Which treatments are recommended for veterans?

The U.S. Department of Veterans Affairs National Center for PTSD recommends eye movement desensitization and reprocessing, cognitive processing therapy, and prolonged exposure therapy as approved trauma treatments for veterans (National Center for PTSD, n.d.-a). This concurs with findings from the 2017 VA/DoD Clinical Practice Guideline for the Management of PTSD (Department of Veterans Affairs & Department of Defense, 2017). The Guideline prioritizes these three treatments because they've produced the strongest evidence of efficacy in reviewed clinical trials. Eye movement desensitization and reprocessing, and prolonged exposure therapy are described in questions 30 and 33, respectively. Both have been extensively studied and have helped many veterans alleviate symptoms of PTSD and take significant steps in their recovery.

Cognitive processing therapy (CPT) begins with psychoeducation about trauma and its effects. It has a strong foundation in cognitive behavioral theory, as much of the work is based around assessment of what survivors' traumatic events have caused them to think and believe. In the early stages of treatment, veterans write an "impact statement." This is described in studies to be an essay on how trauma affected their views about themselves, other people, and the world (see Beck's "cognitive triad" [Beck, Rush, Shaw, & Emery, 1987, p. 188], mentioned in question 8), and on the personal meaning they've derived from their experiences (Sobel, Resick, & Rabalais, 2009). Therapy focuses on helping them identify, access, and express their related emotions, and assess the evidence and context behind these underlying cognitions (Resick et al., 2017). Like other modalities, CPT facilitates healing through the power of a written and verbal narrative. Veterans writing about their traumatic experiences and then reading them aloud allows for processing on multiple levels. It gives the fragmented memory of trauma a means to come together as a structured sequence of events and then reconsolidate within the chronological frame of an autobiographical account. The narrative provides opportunities in therapy for the veteran and therapist to work together in finding the cognitive distortions that trauma caused and sustained. These distortions are weighed against insights and conclusions learned along the way, and veterans come to realize and acquire more adaptive perspectives outside of the trauma's influence. CPT can be provided in individual or group therapy and has a typical duration of 12 weeks. Groups bring the added benefit of meaningful connection between veterans as they support and relate to one another through the treatment (National Center for PTSD, n.d.-b).

When it comes to recommended medication treatment for PTSD, the U.S. Food and Drug Administration has only approved two medications: sertraline (Zoloft) and paroxetine (Paxil) (Alexander, 2012). The aforementioned *VA/DOD Clinical Practice Guideline* (Department of Veterans Affairs & Department of Defense, 2017) offers additional recommendations for veterans. Among monotherapy medication treatments (treatment with a single medication), their strongest recommendations include both sertraline and paroxetine as well as fluoxetine (Prozac) and venlafaxine (Effexor). The Guideline also acknowledges the potential benefit of Prazosin, a blood pressure medication that's been found to help in decreasing nightmares, but doesn't recommend it as a stand-alone treatment.

Additional guidelines and studies have concluded that the combination of psychotherapy and medication treatment can bring an enhanced treatment response for veterans and can result in outcomes better than either intervention by itself (Reisman, 2016).

45. Is it possible to be fully recovered from trauma?

Recovery from trauma is possible. But what does it mean to be "fully recovered"? The question of possibility demands a definition. How would you imagine full recovery? Where would you look for evidence of it? Are you looking at what's been taken from you or at what has survived? The answers won't be found by counting your scars. They're discovered by recognizing the proof of your healing. Scars themselves, in fact, can be testaments to what you've overcome. Open wounds are what fester.

What have you learned about yourself from your recovery so far? If you were offering advice or encouragement to someone who survived something similar, what would you say? We establish a redefinition of what our trauma means about us when we consider not only the pain we endured but also the strength, wisdom, and growth we've discovered from the journey of becoming well. For some people, this is a creation of a new and transformative understanding of themselves and how they choose to live their lives. For others, it looks more like a return to who they once were.

When assessing how far you've come, and what problems remain, be careful not to pathologize the skills that trauma has taught you. Survivors of domestic violence, sexual abuse, or sex trafficking, for example, are often keenly adept at reading people. They've learned to pick up on minute details and changes in others' demeanor and behavior and to adjust their personas to fit the situation. They had to rely upon these skills in order to survive. If these survivors achieve full recovery from trauma, by their definition, they'll probably retain those same abilities. They'll continue to be acutely intuitive, still capable of reading someone like a book, even after they've achieved an internal felt-sense of mental and physical safety. Veterans and first responders who succeed in becoming less hypervigilant tend to maintain their fine-tuned capacity for situational awareness. It's important to remember that the survivor skills we've retained are not evidence against how well we've become. They persist not because they're open wounds but because they're what equipped us to keep living. As resilience builds and our symptoms calm, these skills become something we can draw upon deliberately, on our own terms and without fear. That shift is a confirmation of healing.

Review the answer to question 26. It provides some of the most common ways that survivors reduce their symptoms and ultimately recover from trauma. In questioning whether we've achieved full recovery, the answer depends entirely upon how each of us depicts it. Relief from symptoms is a sure sign of progress, but the reduction or absence of symptoms doesn't necessarily mean that our personal definition has been reached. We're also not by any means exempt from achieving it even when some symptoms remain. There can only be so much finality in our description because we need to account for life continuing to happen. Mental health and wellness don't have an absolute finish line to cross. We're continually faced with new challenges in life and granted endless opportunities for personal growth. The fullness of our recovery is arguably substantiated by our developed resilience for future adversity as much as it is by how effectively we've risen out of the past. It's determined by claiming or reclaiming what trauma has taken from us, and it takes its form as we build our lives beyond its influence. This is where our definition of recovery is truly filled out and brings us to the final question.

46. What is life like after trauma?

Life after trauma is where the realization of recovery is actualized, when the traumatic memories that keep survivors tethered to the past finally give way to the creation of what follows. It's the rise out of the influence of what trauma has taken. The start of this process doesn't need to wait. It can begin in early recovery or at any stage thereafter. The steps that lead to it will vary greatly according to each survivor's values and priorities. Your path to life after trauma will be unique, custom-made to fit your story of growth, and distinguished by the landmarks you create. If you'd like to inform your direction and find guidance when you need to adjust it, you can do so by considering three questions. They sound deceptively simple, but it takes forethought and courage to answer them honestly. They require a willingness to allow for your potential and to dream in the presence of fear, without shutting yourself down with excuses not to do it.

The first question is, As you get well, what changes do you want to make in your life? If your next few chapters amounted to an incredible success story, how would things be different? Would you want to be less isolated and learn to enjoy the company of others? Or to be more independent in some way? Is your goal to have less emotional chaos? Is it to feel safer and more confident, like you're actively living again? Are you interested in finding some way to contribute to helping others? Do you want to experience the joy and creativity you once felt, before it was suffocated and buried by what happened? If you can't remember a time in your life when you had joy and creativity, would you like to discover how it feels?

If answers to the first question don't come easily, they may be shaken loose by considering the second: What if fear, shame, and self-doubt had no bearing on your answer? What changes would you make then? What if you were living without feeling unsafe, unlovable, or not good enough? To answer this, you need to allow for the fact that you're capable of things beyond what you've told yourself and above the standard of how life has treated you. Survivors have sometimes needed to make themselves small to survive. They've needed to retreat into small worlds with routines simplified more and more until daily life finally felt manageable. They sometimes feel estranged from others and believe that recovery is only for people who are "more worthy" of having it. This is the fear that holds us back and prevents us from feeling any sense of future at all. This is the shame carried by shoulders that never deserved the burden. It's self-doubt that will wither and fade as you think outside of trauma's impact and consider the potential that's been hidden beneath it. There is no danger in imagining a future. There's nothing to lose from exercising your creativity, and there's everything to gain by allowing it to become stronger. Creativity and fear can't both win in the same headspace. One pushes the other out. Creativity wins when we learn to give it a voice, and with it comes possibility. As the author and psychologist Thema Bryant-Davis, PhD, tweeted, "When trauma has shaped you, try not to confuse who you had to become with who you can be" (Bryant-Davis, 2019).

The third question is, What would it look like if those changes happened? This requires more thought. It requires detail. If you wanted to be less isolated, what form would that take exactly? How would anyone know you were doing it? How would you, yourself, know? For one person, it may mean gaining one or two or more supportive friendships. For another, it might be joining a support group or reaching out and spending more time with certain family members. Survivors who want less chaos in life may focus on improving their emotion-regulation skills, and that, in turn, might look like fewer crying spells or anger outbursts in any given day or week. That same goal of reducing chaos, for someone else, may be less about self-regulation and more a matter of setting boundaries and distance from toxic relationships. If you'd like to feel more independent or contribute to helping others, your vision could be getting a driver's license, volunteering, part- or full-time employment, or returning to school. Feeling safer and more confident sometimes translates into improving our physical health or getting our own housing. For those living with addiction, a foundation of a life after trauma is based upon sobriety. This is where "recovery" by definition can and should take very different paths. Some people set their sights on reclaiming what trauma has taken from them: the interests and activities they once enjoyed. Others take courageous steps toward attaining what they never had. This third question sharpens your focus on the first and more explicitly spells out the changes that you personally prioritize in your new narrative. If you have difficulty clarifying your intention enough to answer this third question, return to the second one.

Once your direction is charted, recovery is accomplished by the steps you take forward and, equally important, your willingness to get back up when you encounter setbacks. When you're successful in breaking the mold of what life used to look like and you're in the process of casting a new one by your own design, there will be times of uncertainty as you figure it out. The journey begins with a willingness to experiment with what's possible. If the entirety of a goal feels unachievable, consider adding smaller steps. If any of the added steps feel less than achievable when you get to them, add more. Break them down further and further until the railing on the staircase lowers to within your reach. Keep your eye on the change you want, and turn a leap of faith into a series of short hops. Move upward and forward from there. Be patient with yourself, and don't be discouraged by unexpected complications or times of self-doubt. Urges to self-sabotage don't mean you're not cut out for recovery but could be a sign that you're moving too quickly. Take the lesson and slow down without destroying the progress you've made. Amend the plan as you need to. Bring professional and social supports into the fold when they can help, and draw from that support when it's needed.

We come to believe in false ceilings that represent the limits of what we're capable of: ceilings either cast upon us by others or made manifest by what we think about ourselves. We know we're bumping against one when we consider an idea and end with, "Nah. Why bother trying?" Examples may be, "I could never succeed in school" or "I've been out of work too long. Nobody will hire me." They could be, "No relationship is safe" or "Nobody would ever want to spend time with me." These supposed limitations can be very convincing, sometimes right up to the moment we've passed through them. The more distant the goal seems, the more daunting the ceilings feel. We might not even dare to approach them at first. But when we're courageous enough to wonder what lies beyond our expectations, and as we pace ourselves and climb, the view transforms. We start to feel more proficient and confident. We become more resilient. We prove that movement is possible with movement itself, and as we do, the "default" thoughts and beliefs that come into our heads become kinder and much more accurate. We learn to regard our capability with new eyes. Gains in resilience speed the process of recovery, and the process of recovery builds resilience. What once felt impossible and foreign eventually becomes achieved and familiar, and we begin to catch ourselves instinctively making more choices driven by empowerment— choices that we never would have dreamed possible by the view we had from the bottom.

Case Studies

1. THOMAS RECOVERS FROM THE TRAUMA OF SEXUAL ABUSE

Thomas is a seven-year-old boy who's been raised by a single father named Connor. Six weeks ago, Thomas began complaining of stomachaches and was frequently losing his temper. Soon afterward, he started showing unusual and sexualized behaviors. While his father was comforting him and asking about what was happening, Thomas revealed that he was sexually abused by one of his babysitters. Connor contacted the police and scheduled counseling for Thomas shortly thereafter, at the suggestion of his pediatrician. The babysitter was arrested, and criminal proceedings are underway. Thomas has been having regular nightmares and won't fall asleep unless his father is in the room. He's been drawing sexual images and pictures of himself crying, scribbling them out with different colors. He's having trouble focusing at school. When his teacher tries to redirect him to the class activity, Thomas quickly becomes tearful and angry. He's stopped interacting with other children and sits through recess alone.

Connor brings him to a licensed clinical social worker named Hannah, who helps children and their parents with trauma-focused CBT. In the first couple weeks of therapy, Hannah plays games with Thomas, and he begins to feel more comfortable talking with her. She explains to him that she helps kids deal with big worries and feelings, especially after scary things have happened. Connor meets with Hannah as well. They complete the initial assessment, and she introduces him to the process of TF-CBT. He describes the changes that he's seen in Thomas and the kinds of situations that escalate his distress. They discuss common responses to trauma in children, and parenting approaches that Connor can rely upon when his son is anxious or showing aggressive or sexual behavior. Their plan emphasizes positive reinforcement, plenty of father-son time, and Connor's own focus on self-care and use of his supports.

Hannah helps Thomas understand the difference between good touch and inappropriate touch. They identify the safe people in his life, in his family, and at school, those whom he can turn to when he's scared or needs help. They do a series of activities where she shows him how to relax his body and feel better when his tummy becomes upset. They blow bubbles together, and he learns the relaxing effect of controlled breathing and an extended exhale. They watch videos where some of his favorite television characters demonstrate similar exercises. Hannah helps Thomas understand that he's having the same feelings that many other good kids have when they've been through frightening times. They work on naming his feelings, and they talk about how thoughts in our heads can make those feelings change or become stronger. They discuss how our minds can play tricks on us (e.g., self-blame for abuse), especially when we're upset, and how we can relax ourselves and see through those tricks. Thomas's complaints of stomachaches decrease in frequency. His sexualized behaviors are addressed in therapy and otherwise, and they begin to reduce as well.

In the meantime, Hannah is keeping Connor informed about the strategies being used, and he's helping Thomas practice them at home. They're naming sad and angry emotions when Thomas is feeling them, and practicing his techniques for bringing stress down. They're identifying other emotions when they happen, too, like "happy," "silly," and "loved." Connor talks to Thomas's teacher about the coping skills that work best, and she cues him to use them in class when he starts to become upset. She encourages him to play with other kids during recess, and he begins to feel more comfortable joining them. Connor and Hannah also work on improving Thomas's sleep. They establish a consistent routine of reading stories and listening to music before bedtime. They incorporate an in vivo desensitization plan by which Connor gradually decreases his time sitting in Thomas's bedroom as he's falling asleep. He starts by moving to a chair outside Thomas's bedroom door (where Thomas can still see him and with the hallway light on). They then transition to Connor sitting in the hallway within earshot, but out of sight. Thomas's nightmares decrease, and he starts sleeping through the night on his own. Hannah and Thomas make a plan for his narrative. He enjoys drawing, so he makes a picture book about who he is, things he likes to do, and his life before the trauma. The picture book then progresses through the trauma story itself. They practice his relaxation skills through this process, and they name feelings as recalled and felt in session. They go through the story together and watch for "tricks" in his thinking, catching the distortions and correcting them. Thomas's symptoms continue to alleviate as his trauma story is formulated and expressed. Hannah and Connor go over the completed story ahead of time, and the three of them are together when Thomas presents it. Following this conjoint session, Hannah and Thomas review what he's learned and prepare for his discharge from treatment.

Analysis

Thomas shows typical and understandable responses to sexual abuse, including somatic complaints, expression of self-loathing in his drawings, and angry and sexualized behaviors. It's not unusual that he's been isolating from his peers and that his peers are ostracizing him in response to his aggressive behavior. Psychoeducation and treatment are tailored to Thomas at an age-appropriate level. Hannah begins by earning his trust and establishing context about good versus inappropriate touch, an intervention that affirms his right to have that difference respected. She introduces a foundation of self-efficacy, by helping him acknowledge and realize the number of safe people he can turn to if he's upset or needs to feel protected. Connor is included and supported as a participant in his treatment. Together, the team helps Thomas learn how to understand, express, and manage his emotions and reactive thoughts. He gains confidence in his ability to regulate distress in his mind and body, with games and in terms that he can easily understand. Armed with this capability, he's able to work through the story of his trauma. The power of the narrative helps him process and integrate what happened, and sharing it with his father brings the benefit of an elevated level of exposure. Thomas demonstrates the skills and insights he's learned in treatment as he relays his story to the adult that he loves and trusts the most.

2. ASHLEY BUILDS A FOUNDATION OF SAFETY AND SUPPORT

Ashley is a 20-year-old incest survivor who ran away from home when she was 15. She has bounced between living with friends, boyfriends, and strangers for the last several years and has been repeatedly abused emotionally, physically, and sexually. She's earned money from prostitution and selling drugs. Ashley has relied upon cutting her arms for tension relief, and she uses alcohol, benzodiazepines, and heroin in her ongoing effort to "avoid feeling alive." She has been arrested again for possession and agreed to a plea deal that included mental health and substance abuse treatment.

Ashley reports to her addiction counselor that most of the details of her childhood are completely gone from her memory. She starts seeing a psychiatric nurse practitioner, who prescribes her medication, and a case manager, who helps her get housing and support from available assistance programs. She and her treatment team develop a comprehensive plan toward stabilization. Her case manager connects her with a peer support worker who drives her to NA meetings. Ashley works with her addiction counselor on cutting ties with unhealthy people and on understanding and breaking patterns of self-destructive choices. She learns skills for improving distress tolerance, reducing self-harm behaviors, and establishing healthy supports in her life.

Her path to sobriety is marked by big strides and important changes as well as setbacks and times of relapse, and she does her best to learn from every rise and fall. She comes to realize that many of her cravings for drugs come from a drive to self-medicate and escape from her anxiety and the sensations in her body that accompany it. When she's sober, she finds herself dissociating at times, which she recognizes as her mind's effort to protect her from those same feelings. Ashley works on learning body awareness and developing a sense of physical safety through participation in a trauma-sensitive yoga program. She's been carefully approaching the feelings and sensations in her body that she's tried so long to avoid, and mindfully tolerating them for brief periods of time. She's pacing herself carefully, aiming to challenge herself with incremental steps forward without hitting points of overwhelm. Her goal is to build upon the skills she's learned and to solidify her stabilization before processing her trauma experiences more directly in individual therapy.

Analysis

Ashley escaped a household where she had experienced incest and then fought for survival in a world that was equally dangerous. She came to rely upon self-harm and substance use to escape the feelings that she found intolerable, and she was revictimized in patterns of trauma replication. Some of these patterns were maintained in her effort to survive with the only strategies that she knew to rely upon, paired with her exposure to predatory and abusive relationships. Her treatment begins by establishing her safety in housing and equipping her with a means to maintain it without relying upon these unhealthy social connections. She's introduced to survivors she can relate to and begins to develop bonds with new friends who genuinely want to help. As she gains time in sobriety and learns to regulate her emotions, she comes to discover that she can strengthen her resilience by learning to safely attune to her body sensations. Ashley knows her path to recovery will not be a quick fix, but her confidence is strong. She's established a good support system and is moving forward, learning from every step as she goes.

3. KELSEY FACES THE EFFECTS OF CUMULATIVE TRAUMA AS A FIRST RESPONDER

Kelsey is a 29-year-old firefighter and paramedic who was called out to the scene of a car accident almost five months ago. Upon leaving the back of the ambulance and seeing the damaged cars and injured drivers, Kelsey suddenly froze and fell to a crouching position. She was unresponsive when an EMT tried to help her and sat shaking in the road for several minutes before she was finally able to stand and walk back to their vehicle. She's tried to return to work several times since but has found that she can't focus, and she struggles to complete even simple tasks at the station. Nauseating images and memories keep popping into her mind, and she's only been eating one meal per day because her stomach has been "in knots."

Kelsey's sleeping only about five to six hours per night and has been uncharacteristically irritable toward her husband and son. She's been smoking marijuana in an effort to calm her mind and improve her appetite. She explains to loved ones that this whole situation is confusing to her because she's seen a countless number of car accidents in her career, including scenes that she considered more graphic and disturbing than this last one. She's never had this kind of a stress reaction to any of them before now and doesn't understand how a seemingly random ambulance call could do this to her without warning. Kelsey agrees to see a clinician through her employee assistance program, which results in a referral to a therapist who specializes in trauma.

As she and her therapist, Brian, complete an intake assessment, they make a treatment plan to work through her trauma using somatic experiencing therapy. Her stress rises at times when they're discussing her symptoms, and Brian introduces her to exercises she can use to reduce her anxiety. Kelsey finds that these strategies slow her rapid heartbeat and induce physical sensations that bring a sense of safety, confidence, and control. Brian makes her aware of some of the gestures she makes instinctively when she's trying to soothe herself (covering her heart, shaking her legs), and they discuss the meaning and purpose behind these movements. He brings her attention to how she sits and stands most of the time, even when she's not talking about her problems at work (in a collapsed posture, leaning protectively against the nausea in her stomach and the anxiety she feels in her chest, and angling her feet when she sits, like she's about to run for the door).

In exploring these postures and gestures, Kelsey finds that focusing on her body sensations brings some unexpected thoughts and visual images into her mind. She comes to realize that her trauma didn't come entirely from that one single experience with the car accident. It was built over time, with memories piled onto other memories, and feelings she's repeatedly stuffed for the sake of "moving on." Some of these memories involved her time on the job, while others had to do with family life and early events in her childhood, especially when she felt trapped in stressful situations. Brian introduces her to visualization exercises, pairing adaptive and expressive images along with movements that her body instinctively wants to make. Kelsey finds these movements to bring a profound emotional release. She also comes to understand that there were, in fact, several warning signs of her cumulative trauma taking a toll. They came in the form of compromised sleep, compensating with marijuana use at night and large amounts of caffeine in the day, and finding it more and more difficult to "leave work at work." Equipped with this insight and the skills she now has to relax herself, Kelsey's desire to escape these feelings gives way to something she describes as more of a "cautious curiosity" to see what she can learn from them. Her irritability settles, and she is having a much easier time sleeping through the night. Her husband tells her that it's beautiful to see her personality and sense of humor starting to come back.

By pendulating between approaching these memories in discussion and using her resourcing skills, Kelsey is able to process the events she's compartmentalized in her mind and to access and work through the energy that her body devoted to keeping those compartments closed. She experiences a gradual return of her appetite and explains that eating is now much easier because "there are no more bad images popping in into my head."

Analysis

Kelsey copes with her work just as many other first responders learn to do. She does her job and files the stress away, moving on to the next place she's needed and the next task that requires her attention. She's able to continue functioning in her duties for some time, but her mind and body are paying for it behind the scenes. Her sleep becomes disrupted. She finds herself coping with unhealthy quick fixes and struggling more and more to silence the memories and worries that follow her home. There was a pressured energy building within her body that rose beyond the critical threshold of what she could endure, and her mind finally overwhelmed into a more pronounced fight, flight, or freeze response. After removing herself from the situation, and even from the job itself, her mind and body remained stuck in reaction to that overload. Her system was driving an internal imperative for her to run, to fight, to collapse, to do anything necessary to escape the accumulated memories that were violating her internal sense of safety. Kelsey is introduced to several strategies to bring these instinctive responses to completion, to release that energy, and to relax her body out of sympathetic dominance. By gaining insight and applying the skills she's learned, fear is replaced by a cautious curiosity. She's able to process her memories in body and mind, and discharge the trauma within.

4. EMDR HELPS LIAM OVERCOME HIS FEAR OF HIGHWAYS

Liam is a 19-year-old man who was involved in a four-car pileup on a highway during a rainstorm, after the car in front of him hydroplaned. Since then, he's been avoiding driving as much as he can. He's been able to tolerate riding as a passenger on busy roads ("when absolutely necessary") but can only do so if he if he reclines his seat back and keeps his eyes closed for most of the drive. He finds that he can drive by himself for short periods of time but only if he stays on back roads with little to no traffic. The idea of getting on highways accelerates his heart rate and spikes his anxiety, so he avoids them completely. He's come to a mental health center with an interest in medication for anxiety. He agrees to a referral to counseling at the suggestion of his psychiatrist.

Liam meets with a therapist named Jessica who's trained and experienced in the practice of EMDR. Following the initial intake, she introduces him to the basic theory behind this treatment, explains how it may be able to help, and tells him what he can expect from the process. They discuss his routines of self-care and his contact with the supports in his life. Jessica learns that despite his avoidance of driving most of the time, Liam has been doing a great job of staying in touch and spending time with friends and family. She also learns how he's already been challenging himself by driving on back roads, testing the limits of what he can handle.

Jessica and Liam prepare for EMDR by identifying the visual memory he has of the accident, and his related, fear-based beliefs. He explains to her that he's a careful driver but that he feels like being on the road leaves him at the mercy of other drivers' mistakes. He now feels completely unsafe whenever he's in a vehicle. "I know it's excessive, but the feeling is unshakable," he says. They discuss the emotions and stress that he feels when he talks about it and where he feels that stress in his body. Jessica introduces him to resource-installation exercises, which help bring his stress down and effectively contain it. She guides him through relaxing visualizations while he holds onto "pulsers" that vibrate alternately in his hands. Liam finds that while Jessica prompts him on where to place his focus, most of the calming images come from his own mind. She explains that they can use these exercises as needed while they process his trauma with EMDR. They discuss additional relaxation strategies that he can use in session and at home as well.

When they start focusing on the trauma itself, Liam is surprised, at first, at how responsive his mind is to the process. He notices visual memories about the accident coming forward, sometimes vividly, as well as images of what happened before and after. He finds that his stress "waxes and wanes" as his mind revisits what happened, and that the stress he holds in his body plays an important role in understanding the emotions he's feeling. Though he began by describing how he felt paralyzed by the thought of ever driving normally again, he notices, as the weeks go on, that this sense of paralysis is giving way to increasing comfort with the idea of doing it. Jessica encourages him to continue his self-care from week to week, and they set a plan for him to practice more driving between sessions. Liam gradually works his way up to driving on busier roads, and then begins driving short distances on local highways. He starts coming to his sessions smiling, saying that he's "counting exits" and that it's getting easier to go longer distances.

Liam notices that the waves of stress during EMDR continue to vary in intensity at times but are becoming much smaller overall. As they continue with the treatment, the stress finally fades completely. Liam tells Jessica that he understands he can't control other drivers but that he knows he can drive defensively and now feels that he's "reasonably safe" when he does so. His EMDR treatment is complete, and they make a plan to meet every other week for a while as he continues to desensitize and gets more accustomed to driving longer distances on highways.

Analysis

Liam's story illustrates what often happens when someone is traumatized by a car accident. He becomes fearful about driving and avoids it whenever he can. He feels stuck with a persistent feeling that his life is in imminent danger when he's sharing the road with other vehicles. He also knows that driving is necessary, so he tries compensating by practicing on back roads and otherwise catching a ride with someone when he can. While Liam's initial impression is that medication is the only thing that may help, he agrees to try EMDR to see if it works. He's pleased to find that he responds very positively to the treatment. The added component of an in vivo desensitization plan completes the picture and helps him overcome these fears.

5. ALEX HAS PTSD, AND IT'S TAKING A TOLL ON HIS LIFE AND HIS RELATIONSHIP

Alex is a 27-year-old Army veteran who fought overseas, in Iraq, during the second Gulf War. He was able to cope and function effectively for the duration of his service and was honorably discharged. Several weeks after his return, Alex started showing severe symptoms of PTSD. He's been suffering from regular and intrusive memories, including vivid recollections of scanning for signs of IEDs while riding through Iraq, engaging in firefights, and learning shortly after he returned home that one of his fellow soldiers was shot and killed. He's found that the smell of diesel fuel provokes flashbacks, which he describes as "much more real and powerful than any memory could ever be." Alex becomes anxious in large crowds and is highly reactive to the sound of fireworks. He's having terrible nightmares at night and has been losing his temper more frequently during the day.

Alex's relationship is falling apart, and his fiancée, Allison, has been sleeping in a different room. He's repeatedly awakened from nightmares in a burst of panic and anger and at one point started screaming and punching the headboard of their bed. He's reluctant to speak to her about what happened to him overseas because "there's no way she could relate or understand." When Allison tries to comfort him, Alex becomes angry or quiet, both of which leave her feeling "kept at a distance." Alex has been talking and meeting with other veterans. Although he finds it helpful to have people to relate to, he's frequently overcome with feelings of guilt when he thinks about his friend who didn't make it home. He's agreed to participate in a specialized counseling program at the Veterans Affairs clinic.

Alex starts attending VA support groups and also begins individual counseling. He and his therapist use prolonged exposure therapy to process his traumatic experiences and decrease the severity of his PTSD. He's taught skills for relaxing his mind and body and starts a routine of practicing them regularly. Alex recounts his memory of a particular firefight verbally and in great detail, and he tells the narrative repeatedly. His emotions rise to the surface at times, and as they're felt and expressed, he finally begins to feel a sense of closure. He and his therapist record several of his sessions. Alex has one recording that he can listen to if he needs to review the anxiety management skills they discussed. His therapist also records him going through his trauma narrative, and Alex listens to it repeatedly between sessions. He keeps a log when he does this, rating his stress level before, during, and after he listens. He notices the numbers gradually decreasing and then reaching levels much lower than when he started. After completing the treatment with this first narrative, he repeats the process with others. His flashbacks and nightmares decrease in both frequency and intensity. By connecting with other veterans regularly in his support group, Alex is finding it easier to communicate how he feels. Soon afterward, he starts opening up more in conversations with his fiancée. He also begins volunteering to help other veterans who are experiencing trauma symptoms or having difficulty reintegrating back into civilian life. He dedicates this effort to the memory of his fallen friend.

Allison starts attending NAMI (National Alliance on Mental Illness) Homefront meetings, where she learns more about available services for traumatized veterans and their loved ones, and she finds support in talking with other veterans' spouses and families. She joins Alex at times in his individual sessions, where they discuss his progress and her observation of improvements she's seen, as well as his remaining symptoms. They're now planning to start couples counseling, to find ways to strengthen their bond and rebuild their relationship.

Analysis

While some veterans develop PTSD prior to discharge, others sometimes experience pronounced symptoms only after they've returned home from service. There are treatment options for PTSD offered both within the VA system and outside of it, and several modalities can be very effective (see question 44). Support groups offer an opportunity to regain a sense of connection and take risks with communication and vulnerability. This can help build a foundation for practicing those same skills in other relationships. Alex's symptoms brought some serious repercussions and challenges in his relationship with Allison. The NAMI Homefront program is one example of a resource for loved ones who are trying to understand the effects of trauma and find their own support. This case study also shows how personal growth after trauma can be fostered through service to others. Alex's choice to volunteer not only provides benefit for other veterans but also provides him with an opportunity to draw from his experiences and honor the loss of his friend in a productive and meaningful way.

Glossary

Abreaction: Achieving access to the emotions that didn't get a chance to be felt and expressed when trauma occurred, which allows for a cathartic release.

ACE study (CDC-Kaiser Permanente Adverse Childhood Experiences study): A groundbreaking investigation that evaluated how childhood abuse and neglect correlated with increased rates of health problems later in life.

Addictions and Trauma Recovery Integration Model: A 12-week treatment program for addiction and trauma that blends psychoeducation, processing, and expressive activities, with a focus on improving overall health.

Alexithymia: Difficulty perceiving and identifying emotions in ourselves and others.

Allostatic load: The accumulated effects of stress on the body.

Ambivalence: The state of uncertainty and procrastination that we feel when we're considering or planning for changes that contribute to growth and recovery.

Attachment disorders: Conditions that originate in early childhood, particularly when children are exposed to abuse or neglect, don't have consistent caregivers (e.g., children who move from foster home to foster home), or are otherwise adversely affected through their interaction with people responsible for their care.

Bilateral Stimulation: The use of visual, tactile, or auditory stimuli perceived in an alternating, back-and-forth pattern on opposite sides of the body or field of vision.

Borderline personality disorder (BPD): A disorder characterized by maladaptive and deeply rooted patterns of beliefs and behaviors that compromise our ability to function effectively in relationships and in school and work environments. Borderline personality disorder stands out in its relation to trauma because of its theoretical underpinnings in early childhood abuse and neglect, its prevalence in our society, and the extreme suffering that it brings.

Cognitive distortions: Patterns of reactive thoughts and beliefs that influence our perspective and are biased or otherwise inaccurate.

Cognitive processing therapy (CPT): A treatment modality often used with veterans, either individually or in group therapy. It involves creation of an impact statement and trauma narrative as well as assessment and modification of distorted thoughts and beliefs.

Cognitive triad: Beliefs that we've established of ourselves, the people and world around us, and the future. A concept introduced by the psychiatrist Aaron Beck.

Complex trauma: Trauma that results not from an isolated, time-limited event or a relatively finite set of events but rather from a drawn-out and long-term exposure to one or more traumatic circumstances, relationships, or environments.

Depersonalization: A dissociative response that feels like we're perceiving things from outside of ourselves.

Derealization: A dissociative response in which we feel like our surroundings are not authentic but far in the distance or distorted from how we would normally perceive them.

Dialectical behavior therapy (DBT): A modality validated for treatment of borderline personality disorder, often offered in conjoint individual and group therapy, which involves skill-building in mindfulness, distress tolerance, emotion regulation, and interpersonal effectiveness. It was developed by Marsha Linehan, PhD.

Dissociation: A sophisticated defense mechanism by which the brain alleviates distress from trauma by distancing perceptions and feelings from our conscious awareness.

Emotional freedom technique (EFT): An approach, founded by Gary Craig, that involves physically tapping on specific acupressure points.

Evidence-based treatments: Treatment modalities that have been researched, replicated, and tested over time, and have been validated by studies as to their likelihood to be effective.

Eye movement desensitization and reprocessing (EMDR): A psychotherapy modality validated for trauma that utilizes bilateral stimulation of the brain while processing traumatic events. It was developed by Francine Shapiro, PhD.

Fight/flight/freeze response: An automatic physiological survival response to a shocking or threatening event, orchestrated between the brain and the autonomic nervous system.

Flashback: A perceived "reliving" of one or more aspects of a traumatic event. While a flashback is happening, the past and the present no longer feel like two separate experiences.

Grounding: Decreasing the intensity and frequency of dissociative experiences with exercises that cultivate a sense of presence in the here and now, through one or more of the five senses.

Habituation: A natural process in the brain by which the passing of time in a frightening but safe situation lessens our anxiety and helps us become less frightened of it.

Hypnosis: A process by which the conscious mind is induced to profound rest while the subconscious remains attentive and emerges to a more surface level. This process brings us into a trance state, which can be used as a forum for memories to be accessed and related beliefs and drives to be consulted and modified.

Internal family systems (IFS) therapy: A treatment modality that works through understanding and collaboration with the parts of ourselves that protect against our emotional pain from trauma, the parts that carry the burden of that pain, and the core source of our strength and resilience.

Interoception: Awareness and connection to what we feel in our bodies, including how our bodies register stress and emotion.

In vivo desensitization: A means of eliminating phobias and trauma-based anxiety responses to situations that are reasonably safe. It involves a gradual and deliberately paced exposure to the triggering scenario, which causes anxiety to alleviate and allows the mind to adjust to a recognition of safety.

Mentalization therapy: A treatment for borderline personality disorder that introduces ways to learn more adaptive and flexible thinking. It helps improve emotion regulation and relationship skills by recognizing how our perceptions of ourselves relate to our perceptions of others.

Metacognition: Observation and evaluation of our own thought patterns.

Neurofeedback: A means of altering brain wave activity using operant conditioning, that is, modification of mental processes (brain wave activity) by rewarding the brain itself with positive reinforcement.

Neuroplasticity: The capacity for habits and trends that we develop in our thinking to be changed and maintained on a cellular level in the brain. It informs how we perceive and respond to future situations.

Operant conditioning: The modification of behaviors and mental processes using associations with positive reinforcement and/or punishment.

Personality disorders: Deeply rooted patterns of thinking and behavior that are established through childhood and become evident before adolescence or early adulthood. They have a significant negative impact in relationships and in overall life functioning.

Post-traumatic stress disorder (PTSD): A diagnosis commonly given when trauma-related symptoms have been affecting someone significantly for more than a month.

Processing: A term for "working through" what happened (accessing the reactive thoughts, beliefs, and feelings we carry beneath the surface and integrating them consciously), giving release to the emotional charge held in our minds and bodies, and allowing wounds a chance to finally heal.

Prolonged Exposure (PE) therapy: A treatment approach that includes in vivo desensitization, learning skills for decreasing anxiety, and verbally repeating narratives of traumatic experiences. This modality was developed by Edna Foa, PhD.

Reciprocal inhibition: The pairing of focused relaxation with a distressing stimulus.

Recovery: Generally defined in trauma work as relief from trauma-related symptoms and the resolution of the problems they cause in our lives. Beyond that, it is defined and achieved uniquely, according to each survivor's personal beliefs, goals, values, and insights.

Resilience: The durability of our psychological constitution in stressful situations and our ability to adapt to adversity without becoming overwhelmed by it.

Schema therapy: A treatment validated for borderline personality disorder that emphasizes thought assessment and cognitive restructuring, managing distress, and improving interpersonal interaction. It was developed by Jeffrey Young, PhD.

Secondary gains: The often-unspoken reasons "not to get well." They originate from the fear of changes that would come from recovery.

Secondary traumatic stress (also called compassion fatigue): Trauma symptoms caused by witnessing the trauma of others.

Seeking Safety: A treatment model designed by Lisa Najavits, PhD, that helps survivors learn coping skills and establish safety from both addiction and trauma symptoms.

Self-efficacy: Awareness of our own capability and our developed skill set in reaction to problems or crisis, including how we tolerate situations when we don't have the power to change them.

Sensorimotor therapy: A treatment modality developed in collaboration between Pat Ogden, PhD, and Kekuni Minton, PhD, that incorporates sensorimotor (oriented in the senses and motor movement), cognitive, and emotional processing components in its approach for processing trauma.

Social attunement: Our ability to empathize and connect with one another.

Somatic experiencing: A treatment approach that emphasizes interoception, with strategies that allow for reactive trauma responses in the mind and body to be gently encountered and given a means of completion and release. It was developed by Peter A. Levine, PhD.

Somnambulism: A relatively deep state of trance experienced in hypnosis.

Sympathetic dominance: A state in which the sympathetic branch of our autonomic nervous system is primarily and disproportionately activated, causing increased anxiety, release of stress hormones, and a higher level of severity in PTSD symptoms.

Trauma: An experience or series of experiences that is perceived as so distressing, threatening, or shocking that it overwhelms the mind's capacity to effectively process and contain it.

Trauma-focused cognitive behavioral therapy (TF-CBT): A treatment modality validated for trauma of children, adolescents, and older teens. It offers a conjoint approach that includes the survivor's caregiver or another supportive adult in the survivor's life. It was developed by Judith Cohen, MD; Esther Deblinger, PhD; and Anthony Mannarino, PhD.

Trauma narrative: A structured means of expressing the story of what traumatized us.

Trauma recovery and empowerment model (TREM): A group treatment model for women which uses skill building, psychoeducation and social support to help with addiction and recovery from abuse.

Trauma reenactment: Predominantly unconscious replications of environmental or behavioral aspects of a traumatic event.

Traumatic grief: A term used when a grief process has been compounded by a concurrent trauma response to an overwhelming loss.

Trigger: An internal or external reminder of trauma that elicits an anxiety response, often accompanied by memories, sensations, perceptions, and/or emotions associated with what happened.

Directory of Resources

BOOKS

Bass, E., & Davis, L. (2008). *The courage to heal: A guide for women survivors of child sexual abuse.* (20th anniversary ed.). New York, NY: Perennial Library/Harper & Row Publishers.

Copeland, M. E., & Harris, M. (2000). *Healing the trauma of abuse: A women's workbook.* Oakland, CA: New Harbinger Publications.

Levine, P. A. (2008). *Healing trauma: A pioneering program for restoring the wisdom of your body.* Boulder, CO: Sounds True.

Rosenbloom, D., Williams, M. B., & Watkins, B. E. (2010). *Life after trauma, second edition: A workbook for healing.* New York, NY: Guilford Press.

van der Kolk, B. (2014). *The body keeps the score. Brain, mind, and body in the healing of trauma.* New York, NY: Penguin Group.

Vermilyea, E. G. (2013). *Growing beyond survival: A self-help toolkit for managing traumatic stress.* Baltimore, MD: The Sidran Institute Press.

Walker, P. (2013). *Complex PTSD: From surviving to thriving.* Lafayette, CA: Azure Coyote.

Williams, M. B., & Poijula, S. (2016). *The PTSD workbook: Simple, effective techniques for overcoming traumatic stress symptoms.* Oakland, CA: New Harbinger Publications, Inc.

ORGANIZATIONS

National Alliance for Mental Illness. "NAMI provides advocacy, education, support and public awareness so that all individuals and families affected by mental illness can build better lives." http://www.nami.org

National Domestic Violence Hotline. "At the National Domestic Violence Hotline, our highly trained expert advocates are available 24/7 to talk confidentially with anyone in the United States who is experiencing domestic violence, seeking resources or information, or questioning unhealthy aspects of their relationship." https://www.thehotline.org

National Education Alliance for Borderline Personality Disorder. "The mission of National Education Alliance for Borderline Personality Disorder is to provide education, raise public awareness and understanding, decrease stigma, promote research, and enhance the quality of life of those affected by Borderline Personality Disorder and/or related problems, including emotion dysregulation." https://www.borderlinepersonalitydisorder.org

National Suicide Prevention Hotline. "The Lifeline provides 24/7, free and confidential support for people in distress, prevention and crisis resources for you or your loved ones, and best practices for professionals." https://suicidepreventionlifeline.org

Rape, Abuse, & Incest National Network. "RAINN (Rape, Abuse & Incest National Network) is the nation's largest anti-sexual violence organization. RAINN created and operates the National Sexual Assault Hotline (800.656.HOPE) in partnership with more than 1,000 local sexual-assault service providers across the country and operates the DoD Safe Helpline for the Department of Defense. RAINN also carries out programs to prevent sexual violence, help survivors, and ensure that perpetrators are brought to justice." https://www.rainn.org

The Trevor Project. "The Trevor Project is the leading national organization providing crisis intervention and suicide prevention services to lesbian, gay, bisexual, transgender, queer & questioning youth." https://www.thetrevorproject.org

U.S. Department of Veterans Affairs National Center for PTSD. "We are the world's leading research and educational center of excellence on PTSD and traumatic stress." https://www.ptsd.va.gov

VA "Coaching Into Care" Service. "Coaching Into Care is a national telephone service of the VA which aims to educate, support, and empower family members and friends who are seeking care or services for a Veteran." https://www.mirecc.va.gov/coaching

WEBSITES

These websites include directories to find clinicians trained in the following treatment modalities:

Cognitive Processing Therapy
https://cptforptsd.com

Dialectical Behavior Therapy
https://dbt-lbc.org

Eye Movement Desensitization and Reprocessing
http://www.emdr.com
http://www.emdria.org

Internal Family Systems Therapy
http://www.ifs-institute.com

Prolonged Exposure Therapy
https://www.med.upenn.edu/ctsa/find_pe_therapist.html

Schema Therapy
https://schematherapysociety.org

Sensorimotor Psychotherapy
https://www.sensorimotorpsychotherapy.org

Somatic Experiencing
https://traumahealing.org

Trauma-Focused Cognitive Behavioral Therapy
http://www.tfcbt.org

❖

Bibliography

INTRODUCTION

1. Kluger, J. (2010, May 10). The 2010 TIME 100. Thinkers. Edna Foa. *Time, 175*(18).

QUESTION 1

1. Zimbardo, P., Sword, R., & Sword, R. (2012). *The time cure: Overcoming PTSD with the new psychology of time perspective therapy.* San Francisco, CA: Jossey-Bass.
2. Sherin, J. E., & Nemeroff, C. B. (2011). Post-traumatic stress disorder: The neurobiological impact of psychological trauma. *Dialogues in Clinical Neuroscience, 13*(3), 263–278. Retrieved from https://www.ncbi.nlm.nih.gov/pmc/articles/PMC3182008
3. Morey, R. A., Haswell, C. C., Hooper, S. R., & De Bellis, M. D. (2016). Amygdala, hippocampus, and ventral medial prefrontal cortex volumes differ in maltreated youth with and without chronic post-traumatic stress disorder. *Neuropsychopharmacology, 41*(3), 791–801.

QUESTION 2

1. American Psychiatric Association. (2013). *Diagnostic and statistical manual of mental disorders* (5th ed.). Arlington, VA: Author.
2. Levy, K. N., Johnson, B. N., Clouthier, T. L., Scala, J. W., & Temes, C. M. (2015). An attachment theoretical framework for personality

disorders. *Canadian Psychology/Psychologie Canadienne*, 56(2), 197–207. Retrieved from https://www.apa.org/pubs/journals/features/cap-0000025.pdf

QUESTION 3

1. Zero to Six Collaborative Group, National Child Traumatic Stress Network. (2010). *Early childhood trauma.* Los Angeles, CA: National Center for Child Traumatic Stress. Retrieved from https://www.nctsn.org/sites/default/files/resources/early_childhood_trauma.pdf
2. PTSD: National Center for PTSD. (2019a, October 17). How common is PTSD in children and teens? Retrieved from https://www.ptsd.va.gov/understand/common/common_children_teens.asp
3. PTSD: National Center for PTSD. (2019b, October 17). How common is PTSD in adults? Retrieved from https://www.ptsd.va.gov/understand/common/common_adults.asp
4. Greene, T., Neria, Y., & Gross, R. (2016). Prevalence, detection and correlates of PTSD in the primary care setting: A systematic review. *Journal of Clinical Psychology in Medical Settings*, 23, 160–180. Retrieved from http://hw.haifa.ac.il/images/stories/files/menthal_health/year_2015_2016/Puplication/PTSD_primary_care.pdf

QUESTION 4

1. Perpetrators of Sexual Violence: Statistics. (n.d.). Retrieved from RAINN website: https://www.rainn.org/statistics/perpetrators-sexual-violence
2. Khaleque, A. (2015). Perceived parental neglect, and children's psychological maladjustment, and negative personality dispositions: A meta-analysis of multi-cultural studies. *Journal of Child and Family Studies*, 24(5), 1419–1428.
3. Mayer, M., Lavergne, C., Tourigny, M., & Wright, J. (2007). Characteristics differentiating neglected children from other reported children. *Journal of Family Violence*, 22(8), 721–732.

QUESTION 5

1. Belsky, J., & Domitrovich, C. (1997). Temperament and parenting antecedents of individual difference in three-year-old boys' pride and shame reactions. *Child Development*, 68(3), 456–466.
2. NCADV: National Coalition against Domestic Violence Statistics. (n.d.). Retrieved from https://ncadv.org/statistics
3. NCTSN: National Child Traumatic Stress Network. (n.d.) Questions and answers about domestic violence: An interview with Betsy

McAlister Groves. Retrieved from https://www.nctsn.org/sites/default/files/resources//questions_answers_about_domestic_violence.pdf

4. NCTSN: National Child Traumatic Stress Network. (2018, October 17). *Intimate partner violence and child trauma: Policy brief*. Retrieved from https://www.nctsn.org/resources/intimate-partner-violence-and-child-trauma-policy-brief

5. Anders, C. J. (2015, December 16). From "irritable heart" to "shell-shock": How post-traumatic stress became a disease. Retrieved from https://io9.gizmodo.com/from-irritable-heart-to-shellshock-how-post-trauma-5898560

6. Simiola, V., & Norman, S. (n.d.). Underserved populations: Trauma and post-traumatic stress disorder in veterans. Retrieved from https://www.apatraumadivision.org/633/resources-on-underserved-populations.html

7. Junger, S. (2015, May 7). How PTSD became a problem far beyond the battlefield. *Vanity Fair*. Retrieved from https://www.vanityfair.com/news/2015/05/ptsd-war-home-sebastian-junger

8. Junger, S. (n.d.). Our lonely society makes it hard to come home from war. Retrieved from https://www.ted.com/talks/sebastian_junger_our_lonely_society_makes_it_hard_to_come_home_from_war

9. Department of Veterans Affairs, Veterans Health Administration, Office of Mental Health and Suicide Prevention. (2018, September). *Veteran suicide data report, 2005–2016*. Retrieved from https://www.mentalhealth.va.gov/docs/data-sheets/OMHSP_National_Suicide_Data_Report_2005-2016_508.pdf

10. PTSD: National Center for PTSD. (2018, July 24). How common is PTSD in veterans? Retrieved from https://www.ptsd.va.gov/understand/common/common_veterans.asp

11. Morral, A. R., Gore, K., Schell, T. L., Bicksler, B., Farris, C., Ghosh-Dastidar, B., ... Williams, K. M. (2015, May 1). Sexual Assault and Sexual Harassment in the U.S. Military. Retrieved from RAND website: https://www.rand.org/pubs/research_briefs/RB9841.html

12. Campus Sexual Violence: Statistics. (n.d.). Retrieved from RAINN website: https://www.rainn.org/statistics/campus-sexual-violence

13. McCauley, J. L., Killeen, T., Gros, D. F., Brady, K. T., & Back, S. E. (2012, September). Post-traumatic stress disorder and co-occurring substance use disorders: Advances in assessment and treatment. *Clinical Psychology, 19*(3), 283–304. doi:10.1111/cpsp.12006

14. Kosciw, J. G., Greytak, E. A., Giga, N. M., Villenas, C., & Danischewski, D. (2016). *2015 national school climate survey: The experiences of lesbian, gay, bisexual, transgender and queer youth in our nation's*

schools. New York, NY: GLSEN. Retrieved from GLSEN website: https://www.glsen.org/sites/default/files/2015%20National%20 GLSEN%202015%20National%20School%20Climate%20 Survey%20%28NSCS%29%20-%20Full%20Report_0.pdf

15. Facts about Suicide. (n.d.). Retrieved from the Trevor Project website: https://www.thetrevorproject.org/resources/preventing-suicide /facts-about-suicide/#sm.0001lemmi2cxlfqypoe14ydylwr4p

16. Leomporra, A., & Hustings, M. (Eds.). (2018). *Vulnerable to hate: A survey of bias-motivated violence against people experiencing homelessness in 2016–2017*. Retrieved from the National Coalition for the Homeless website: https://nationalhomeless.org/wp-content/uploads/2018/12 /hate-crimes-2016-17-final_for-web.pdf

17. Meinbresse, M., Brinkley-Rubinstein, L., Grassette, A., Benson, J., Hall, C., Hamilton, R., . . . Jenkins, D. M. (2014). Exploring the experiences of violence among individuals who are homeless using a consumer-led approach. *Violence and Victims, 29*(1), 122–136. Retrieved from https://www.nhchc.org/wp-content/uploads/2014/08/vv-29-1_ptr _a8_122-136.pdf

18. Missing Children Statistics. (n.d.). Retrieved from NCMEC, National Center for Missing & Exploited Children, website: http://www .missingkids.com/footer/media/keyfacts#missingchildrenstatistics

19. Silove, D., Ventevogel, P., & Rees, S. (2017). The contemporary refugee crisis: An overview of mental health challenges. *World Psychiatry, 16*(2), 130–139. doi:10.1002/wps.20438

20. Levy-Gigi, E., Richter-Levin, G., & Kéri, S. (2014). The hidden price of repeated traumatic exposure: Different cognitive deficits in different first-responders. *Frontiers in Behavioral Neuroscience*, 8, article 281. doi:10.3389/fnbeh.2014.00281

21. ACS-NYU Children's Trauma Institute. (2012). *Addressing secondary traumatic stress among child welfare staff: A practice brief*. Retrieved from National Child Traumatic Stress Network website: https:// www.nctsn.org/sites/default/files/resources/fact-sheet/addressing_sts_ among_child_welfare_staff_a_practice_brief.pdf

22. Haney, C. (2001). *From prison to home: The effect of incarceration and reentry on children, families and communities*. Retrieved from the U.S. Department of Health & Human Services website: https:// aspe.hhs.gov/basic-report/psychological-impact-incarceration- implications-post-prison-adjustment

23. Wolff, N., & Shi, J. (2012). Childhood and adult trauma experiences of incarcerated persons and their relationship to adult behavioral health problems and treatment. *International Journal of Environmental Research and Public Health, 9*(5), 1908–1926. doi:10.3390/ijerph9051908

QUESTION 6

1. van der Kolk, B. (2014). *The body keeps the score. Brain, mind, and body in the healing of trauma.* New York, NY: Penguin Group.
2. Porges, S. W. (2009). The polyvagal theory: New insights into adaptive reactions of the autonomic nervous system. *Cleveland Clinic Journal of Medicine, 76*(Supplement 2), S86–S90. doi:10.3949/ccjm.76.s2.17
3. Porges, S. W. (2003). Social engagement and attachment: A phylogenetic perspective. *Annals of the New York Academy of Sciences, 1008,* 31–47. Retrieved from http://condor.depaul.edu/dallbrit/extra/psy588/porges-NYAS.pdf

QUESTION 8

1. Beck, A. T., Rush, A. J., Shaw, B. E., & Emery, G. (1987). *Cognitive therapy of depression.* The Guilford clinical psychology and psychopathology series. New York, NY: Guilford Press.

QUESTION 9

1. Bridge, D. J., & Paller, K. A. (2012). Neural correlates of reactivation and retrieval-induced distortion. *The Journal of Neuroscience, 32*(35), 12144–12151. doi:10.1523/JNEUROSCI.1378-12.2012
2. Bedard-Gilligan, M., Zoellner, L. A., & Feeny, N. C. (2017). Is trauma memory special? Trauma narrative fragmentation in PTSD: Effects of treatment and response. *Clinical Psychological Science: A Journal of the Association for Psychological Science, 5*(2), 212–225. doi:10.1177/2167702616676581
3. Alhola, P., & Polo-Kantola, P. (2007). Sleep deprivation: Impact on cognitive performance. *Neuropsychiatric Disease and Treatment, 3*(5), 553–567. Retrieved from https://www.ncbi.nlm.nih.gov/pmc/articles/PMC2656292

QUESTION 10

1. Pan, X., Kaminga, A. C., Wen, S. W., & Liu, A. (2018). Catecholamines in post-traumatic stress disorder: A systematic review and meta-analysis. *Frontiers in Molecular Neuroscience, 11,* article 450. doi:10.3389/fnmol.2018.00450
2. Danese, A., & McEwen, B. S. (2012). Adverse childhood experiences, allostasis, allostatic load, and age-related disease. *Physiology & Behavior, 106*(1), 29–39. Retrieved from https://www.acesconnection.com/fileSendAction/fcType/0/fcOid/423235373905059800/filePointer/423235373931506913/fodoid/423235373931506909/Bruce%20MC.pdf

3. About the CDC-Kaiser ACE Study. (n.d.). Retrieved from https://www
   .cdc.gov/violenceprevention/childabuseandneglect/acestudy/about
   .html
4. Got Your ACE Score? (2018, July 10). *ACESTooHigh*. Retrieved
   from https://acestoohigh.com/got-your-ace-score
5. Felitti, V. J., Anda, R. F., Nordenberg, D., Williamson, D. F., Spitz,
   A. M., Edwards, V., . . . Marks, J. S. (1998). Relationship of childhood
   abuse and household dysfunction to many of the leading causes of
   death in adults: The Adverse Childhood Experiences (ACE) study.
   American Journal of Preventive Medicine, 14(4), 245–258. Retrieved
   from doi:10.1016/S0749-3797(98)00017-8
6. Kelly-Irving, M., Lepage, B., Dedieu, D., Bartley, M., Blane, D., Gro-
   sclaude, P., . . . Delpierre, C. (2013). Adverse childhood experiences
   and premature all-cause mortality. *European Journal of Epidemiology,
   28*(9), 721–734. doi:10.1007/s10654-013-9832-9
7. Traub, F., & Boynton-Jarrett, R. (2017). Modifiable resilience factors to childhood adversity for clinical pediatric practice. *Pediatrics,
   139*(5), e20162569. doi:10.1542/peds.2016-2569
8. Spencer-Hwang, R., Torres, X., Valladares, J., Pasco-Rubio, M.,
   Dougherty, M., & Kim, W. (2018, Spring). Childhood experiences
   among a community of resilient centenarians and seniors: Implications for a chronic disease prevention framework. *The Permanente
   Journal, 22*, 17–146. doi:10.7812/TPP/17-146

QUESTION 11

1. Borg, E. R., & Chavez, B. (2014, May). Psychotropic-induced sexual
   dysfunction. *Mental Health Clinician, 4*(3), 138–145. doi:10.9740/mhc
   .n197919

QUESTION 12

1. Brewin, C. R. (2014). Episodic memory, perceptual memory, and
   their interaction: Foundations for a theory of post-traumatic stress
   disorder. *Psychological Bulletin, 140*, 69–97. doi:10.1037/a0033722
2. Ehlers, A., Hackmann, A., & Michael, T. (2004). Intrusive re-experiencing
   in post-traumatic stress disorder: Phenomenology, theory, and therapy.
   Memory, 12(4), 403–415. doi:10.1080/09658210444000025
3. Lanius, R. A., Williamson, P. C., Densmore, M., Boksman, K., Neufeld,
   R. W., Gati, J. S., & Menon, R. S. (2004). The nature of traumatic
   memories: A 4-T fMRI functional connectivity analysis. *The American
   Journal of Psychiatry, 161*(1), 36–44. doi:10.1176/appi.ajp.161.1.36

QUESTION 13

1. Greenberg, N., Brooks, S., & Dunn, R. (2015). Latest developments in post-traumatic stress disorder: Diagnosis and treatment. *British Medical Bulletin, 114*(1), 147–155. doi:10.1093/bmb/ldv014

2. Carlson, E. B., Dalenberg, C., & McDade-Montez, E. (2012). Dissociation in post-traumatic stress disorder part 1: Definitions and review of research. *Psychological Trauma: Theory, Research, Practice, and Policy, 4*(5), 479–489. doi:10.1037/a0027748

QUESTION 14

1. American Psychiatric Association. (2013). *Diagnostic and statistical manual of mental disorders* (5th ed.). Arlington, VA: Author.

2. Stone, M. H. (1977). The borderline syndrome: Evolution of the term, genetic aspects, and prognosis. *American Journal of Psychotherapy, 31*(3), 345–365.

3. Harvard Health Publishing. (2006, June). Borderline personality disorder: Origins and symptoms. Retrieved from https://www.health.harvard.edu/newsletter_article/Borderline_personality_disorder_Origins_and_symptoms

4. Personality Disorders. (n.d.). Retrieved from the National Institute of Mental Health website: https://www.nimh.nih.gov/health/statistics/personality-disorders.shtml

5. Crowell, S. E., Beauchaine, T. P., & Linehan, M. M. (2009). A biosocial developmental model of borderline personality: Elaborating and extending Linehan's theory. *Psychological Bulletin, 135*(3), 495–510. doi:10.1037/a0015616

6. Linehan, M. (1993). *Cognitive-behavioral treatment of borderline personality disorder*. New York, NY: Guilford Press.

7. Borderline Personality Disorder. (n.d.). Retrieved from the National Institute of Mental Health website: https://www.nimh.nih.gov/health/publications/borderline-personality-disorder/index.shtml

8. Reichborn-Kjennerud, T. (2010). The genetic epidemiology of personality disorders. *Dialogues in Clinical Neuroscience, 12*(1), 103–114. Retrieved from https://www.ncbi.nlm.nih.gov/pmc/articles/PMC3181941

9. Biological Factors Related to the Development of Personality Disorders (Nature). (n.d.). Retrieved August 6, 2019, from https://www.mentalhelp.net/articles/biological-factors-related-to-the-development-of-personality-disorders-nature

QUESTION 16

1. Morgan, O. J. (2009). Thoughts on the interaction of trauma, addiction, and spirituality. *Journal of Addictions & Offender Counseling*, 30(1), 5–15.

2. Wu, N. S., Schairer, L. C., Dellor, E., & Grella, C. (2010). Childhood trauma and health outcomes in adults with comorbid substance abuse and mental health disorders. *Addictive Behaviors*, 35(1), 68–71. doi:10 .1016/j.addbeh.2009.09.003

3. Craparo, G., Ardino, V., Gori, A., & Caretti, V. (2014). The relationships between early trauma, dissociation, and alexithymia in alcohol addiction. *Psychiatry Investigation*, 11(3), 330–335. doi:10.4306/pi .2014.11.3.330

4. Ford, J. D., & Russo, E. (2006). Trauma-focused, present-centered, emotional self-regulation approach to integrated treatment for post-traumatic stress and addiction: Trauma adaptive recovery group education and therapy (TARGET). *American Journal of Psychotherapy*, 60(4), 335–355. Retrieved from https://www.cttntraumatraining.org /uploads/4/6/2/3/46231093/target-am_j_psychotherapy.pdf

5. Kim, B., Nolan, S., & Ti, L. (2017). Addressing the prescription opioid crisis: Potential for hospital based interventions? *Drug and Alcohol Review*, 36(2), 149–152.

6. About Seeking Safety. (n.d.). Retrieved from the Seeking Safety website: https://www.treatment-innovations.org/ss-description.html

7. Lenz, A. S., Henesy, R., & Callender, K. (2016). Effectiveness of seeking safety for co-occurring post-traumatic stress disorder and substance use. *Journal of Counseling & Development*, 94, 51–61. Retrieved from https://www.treatment-innovations.org/uploads/2/5/5/5/25555853 /2016_lenz_et_al_meta-analysis_of_ss.pdf

8. Conduent Healthy Communities Institute. (n.d.). Trauma Recovery and Empowerment Model (TREM). Retrieved from http://cdc.thehcn .net/promisepractice/index/view?pid=864

9. Substance Abuse and Mental Health Services Administration. (2014). *Trauma-informed care in behavioral health services*. (Treatment Improvement Protocol [TIP] series 57. HHS Publication No. [SMA] 13-4801). Rockville, MD: Substance Abuse and Mental Health Services Administration. Retrieved fromhttps://www.ncbi.nlm.nih.gov /books/NBK207201/

10. Giordano, A. L., Prosek, E. A., Stamman, J., Callahan, M. M., Loseu, S., Bevly, C. M., Cross, K., . . . Chadwell, K. (2016). Addressing trauma in substance abuse treatment. *Journal of Alcohol and Drug Education*, 60(2), 55–71.

QUESTION 17

1. Ardino, V. (2012). Offending behaviour: The role of trauma and PTSD. *European Journal of Psychotraumatology, 3*(1). doi:10.3402/ejpt .v3i0.18968

2. Early Childhood Victimization among Incarcerated Adult Male Felons. (n.d.). Retrieved from the National Criminal Justice Reference Service website: https://www.ncjrs.gov/pdffiles/fs000204.pdf

3. Plummer, M., & Cossins, A. (2018). The cycle of abuse: When victims become offenders. *Trauma, Violence, & Abuse, 19*(3), 286–304. doi:10.1177/1524838016659487

4. U.S. General Accounting Office. (1996, September). *Cycle of sexual abuse: Research inconclusive about whether child victims become adult abusers.* (GAO/GGD-96-178). Washington, DC: GAO. Retrieved from https://www.gao.gov/assets/230/223155.pdf

5. Richman, M. (2018, September 7). Veterans and the criminal justice system. Retrieved from the U.S. Department of Veterans Affairs Office of Research & Development website: https://www.research.va .gov/currents/0918-VA-researcher-examines-Vets-who-collide-with -criminal-justice-system.cfm

QUESTION 18

1. Ports, K. A., Ford, D. C., & Merrick, M. T. (2016). Adverse childhood experiences and sexual victimization in adulthood. *Child Abuse & Neglect, 51,* 313–322. doi:10.1016/j.chiabu.2015.08.017

2. UNICEF. (2006). *Behind closed doors: The impact of domestic violence on children.* Retrieved from http://www.unicef.org/protection/files /BehindClosedDoors.pdf

3. Whitfield, C. L., Anda, R. F., Dube, S.R., & Felitti, V. J. (2003). Violent childhood experiences and the risk of intimate partner violence in adults: Assessment in a large health maintenance organization. *Journal of Interpersonal Violence, 18,* 166–185. Retrieved from http://www.theannainstitute.org/ACE%20folder%20for%20 website/54%20ACEs%20+%20DV.pdf

4. Contractor, A. A., Weiss, N. H., Dranger, P., Ruggero, C., & Armour, C. (2017). PTSD's risky behavior criterion: Relation with *DSM–5* PTSD symptom clusters and psychopathology. *Psychiatry Research, 252,* 215–222. doi:10.1016/j.psychres.2017.03.008

5. Substance Abuse and Mental Health Services Administration. (2014). *Trauma-informed care in behavioral health services.* (Treatment Improvement Protocol [TIP] series 57. HHS Publication No. [SMA] 13-4801). Rockville, MD: Substance Abuse and Mental Health

Services Administration. Retrieved from https://www.ncbi.nlm.nih
.gov/books/NBK207201/pdf/Bookshelf_NBK207201.pdf

6. van der Kolk, B. A. (1989). The compulsion to repeat the trauma: Re-enactment, revictimization, and masochism. *Psychiatric Clinics of North America, 12*(2), 389–411. Retrieved from http://www.cirp.org /library/psych/vanderkolk/#n120

7. Levy, M. S. (1998). A helpful way to conceptualize and understand reenactments. *The Journal of Psychotherapy Practice and Research, 7*(3), 227–235. Retrieved from https://www.ncbi.nlm.nih.gov/pmc/articles /PMC3330499

QUESTION 19

1. Jennings, A. (2004). The damaging consequences of violence and trauma: Facts, discussion points, and recommendations for the behavioral health system. Retrieved from The Anna Institute website: http:// www.theannainstitute.org/Damaging%20Consequences.pdf%20%20

2. U.S. General Accounting Office. (1996, September). *Cycle of sexual abuse: Research inconclusive about whether child victims become adult abusers.* (GAO/GGD-96-178). Washington, DC: GAO. Retrieved from https://www.gao.gov/assets/230/223155.pdf

3. Brown, M. J., Masho, S. W., Perera, R. A., Mezuk, B., & Cohen, S. A. (2015). Sex and sexual orientation disparities in adverse childhood experiences and early age at sexual debut in the United States: Results from a nationally representative sample. *Child Abuse & Neglect, 46,* 89–102. doi:10.1016/j.chiabu.2015.02.019

QUESTION 20

1. National Collaborating Centre for Mental Health. (2005). *Post-traumatic stress disorder: The management of PTSD in adults and children disorder: The management of PTSD in adults and children in primary and secondary care.* (NICE Clinical Guideline 26). Leicester, United Kingdom: Gaskell. Retrieved from https://www.ncbi.nlm.nih.gov /books/NBK56506

2. The Impact of Trauma. (n.d.). Retrieved from the TeachTrauma website: http://www.teachtrauma.com/information-about-trauma/impact -of-trauma

3. Facts about PTSD and Veterans. (n.d.). Retrieved from https:// unbrokenwarriors.org/ptsd/facts/

4. Wang, C., & Holton, J. (2007). Total estimated costs of child abuse and neglect in the United States. Retrieved from the No Excuse for Child Abuse in America website: http://noexcuseforchildabuseinamerica .com/resources/Economic+Impact+Study+Cost+Of+Child+Abuse.pdf

5. Fang, X., Brown, D. S., Florence, C. S., & Mercy, J. A. (2012). The economic burden of child maltreatment in the United States and implications for prevention. *Child Abuse & Neglect, 36*(2), 156–165. Retrieved from https://www.sciencedirect.com/science/article/pii/S0145213411003140

6. Adams, E. J. (2010). *Healing invisible wounds: Why investing in trauma-informed care for children makes sense* (Justice Policy Institute Policy Brief). Retrieved from http://www.justicepolicy.org/uploads/justicepolicy/documents/10-07_rep_healinginvisiblewounds_jj-ps.pdf

7. Dolezl, T., McCollum, D., & Callahan, M. (2009). *Hidden costs in health care: The economic impact of violence and abuse.* Eden Prairie, MN: Academy on Violence and Abuse. Retrieved from http://www.ccasa.org/wp-content/uploads/2014/01/Economic-Cost-of-VAW.pdf

8. Briggs, E. C., Fairbank, J. A., Greeson, J. K. P., Layne, C. M., Steinberg, A. M., Amaya-Jackson, L. M., . . . Pynoos, R. S. (2012, March 26). Links between child and adolescent trauma exposure and service use histories in a national clinic-referred sample. *Psychological Trauma: Theory, Research, Practice, and Policy*, advance online publication. doi:10.1037/a0027312

QUESTION 22

1. Ceunen, E., Vlaeyen, J. W., & Van Diest, I. (2016). On the origin of interoception. *Frontiers in Psychology, 7*, article 743. doi:10.3389/fpsyg.2016.00743

2. Bonanno, G. A., Galea, S., Bucciarelli, A., & Vlahov, D. (2007). What predicts psychological resilience after disaster? The role of demographics, resources, and life stress. *Journal of Consulting and Clinical Psychology, 75*, 671–682. Retrieved from https://deepblue.lib.umich.edu/bitstream/handle/2027.42/56241/bonanno_what%20predicts%20psychological%20resilience%20after%20disaster_2007.pdf

QUESTION 23

1. Gentry, J. E., Baranowsky, A. B., & Rhoton, R. (2017). Trauma competency: An active ingredients approach to treating post-traumatic stress disorder. *Journal of Counseling & Development, 95*, 279–287. doi:10./1002/jcad.12142

2. Gentry, J. E., & Baranowsky, A. B. (2013). Compassion fatigue resiliency: A new attitude. Retrieved from the Traumatology Institute website: https://psychink.com/ti2012/wp-content/uploads/2013/10/Compassion-Resiliency-A-New-Attitude.pdf

3. Hanson, R., & Mendius, R. (2009). *Buddha's brain: The practical neuroscience of happiness, love & wisdom.* Oakland, CA: New Harbinger Publications.

QUESTION 25

1. Gladwell, M. (2013). *David and Goliath: Underdogs, misfits, and the art of battling giants*. New York, NY: Little, Brown and Company.
2. LaPierre, J. (2019). To the men who step up. Retrieved from the Recovery Rocks website: https://recoveryrocks.bangordailynews.com /2019/06/16/addiction/to-the-men-who-step-up

QUESTION 30

1. Shapiro, F., & Forrest, M. S. (2004). *EMDR: The breakthrough therapy for overcoming anxiety, stress, and trauma*. New York, NY: Basic Books.
2. Grand, D. (2013). *Brainspotting: The revolutionary new therapy for rapid and effective change*. Boulder, CO: Sounds True.
3. The Flash Technique. (n.d.). Retrieved from https://flashtechnique .com
4. EMDR Institute. (n.d.). Providing an effective therapy for the treatment of trauma. Retrieved from http://www.emdr.com

QUESTION 31

1. Cohen, J. A., Mannarino, A. P., & Deblinger, E. (2017). *Treating trauma and traumatic grief in children and adolescents* (2nd ed.). New York, NY: Guilford Press.
2. TF-CBT Training Package. (2019, October 23). Retrieved from https://tfcbt.org/training/tf-cbt-training-package-13

QUESTION 33

1. Rothbaum, B. O., Foa, E. B., & Hembree, E. A. (2007). *Treatments that work. Reclaiming your life from a traumatic experience: Workbook*. Oxford: Oxford University Press.

QUESTION 34

1. Schwartz, R. C., & Sweezy, M. (2020). *Internal family systems therapy* (2nd ed.). New York, NY: Guilford Press.

QUESTION 36

1. Neurofeedback. (n.d.). Retrieved from the Trauma Center at Justice Resource Institute website: http://www.traumacenter.org/clients /neurofeedback.php

QUESTION 37

1. Levine, P. A. (1997). *Waking the tiger: Healing trauma*. Berkeley, CA: North Atlantic Book.

2. Brom, D., Stokar, Y., Lawi, C., Nuriel-Porat, V., Ziv, Y., Lerner, K., & Ross, G. (2017). Somatic experiencing for post-traumatic stress disorder: A randomized controlled outcome study. *Journal of Traumatic Stress, 30*(3), 304–312. doi:10.1002/jts.22189

3. Payne, P., Levine, P. A., & Crane-Godreau, M. A. (2015). Somatic experiencing: Using interoception and proprioception as core elements of trauma therapy. *Frontiers in Psychology,* 6, article 93. doi:10.3389/fpsyg.2015.00093

4. Ogden, P., & Minton, K. (2000). Sensorimotor psychotherapy: One method for processing traumatic memory. *Traumatology, 7,* 1–20. Retrieved from https://www.sensorimotorpsychotherapy.org/articles.html

5. Ogden, P., & Fisher, J. (2016). *Sensorimotor psychotherapy: Interventions for trauma and attachment.* New York, NY: W. W. Norton.

QUESTION 38

1. Alexander, W. (2012). Pharmacotherapy for post-traumatic stress disorder in combat veterans: Focus on antidepressants and atypical antipsychotic agents. *P & T, 37*(1), 32–38. Retrieved from https://www.ncbi.nlm.nih.gov/pmc/articles/PMC3278188

2. PTSD: National Center for PTSD. (n.d.-a). Medications for PTSD. Retrieved from https://www.ptsd.va.gov/understand_tx/meds_for_ptsd.asp

3. PTSD: National Center for PTSD. (n.d.-b). Benzodiazepines and PTSD. Retrieved from https://www.ptsd.va.gov/understand_tx/benzos_ptsd.asp

4. Whitaker, B. (2019). SGB: A possible breakthrough treatment for PTSD. Retrieved from the CBS News website: https://www.cbsnews.com/news/sgb-a-possible-breakthrough-treatment-for-ptsd-60-minutes-2019-06-16

5. Abbott, H., & Polevoy, M. (2019, November 7). New Army-funded research shows promise for PTSD treatment featured on 60 Minutes. Retrieved from the CBS News website: https://www.cbsnews.com/news/sgb-for-ptsd-new-army-funded-research-shows-promise-for-ptsd-treatment-featured-on-60-minutes

QUESTION 39

1. van der Kolk, B. A., Stone, L., West, J., Rhodes, A., Emerson, D., Suvak, M, & Spinazzola, J. (2014). Yoga as an adjunctive treatment for post-traumatic stress disorder: A randomized controlled trial. *Journal of Clinical Psychiatry, 75*(6), e559–e565. doi:10.4088/JCP.13m08561

2. Clark, C. J., Lewis-Dmello, A., Anders, D., Parsons, A., Nguyen-Feng, V., Henn, L., & Emerson, D. (2014). Trauma-sensitive yoga as an adjunct mental health treatment in group therapy for survivors of domestic violence: A feasibility study. *Complementary Therapies in Clinical Practice, 20*(3), 152–158. doi:10.1016/j.ctcp.2014.04.003

3. Trauma Center. (n.d.). History of TCTSY. Retrieved from https://www.traumasensitiveyoga.com/history-of-tctsy.html

4. Helms, J. (1998). An overview of medical acupuncture. *Alternative Therapies in Health and Medicine, 4*, 35–45. Retrieved from the American Academy of Medical Acupuncture website: http://www.medicalacupuncture.org/For-Patients/Articles-By-Physicians-About-Acupuncture/An-Overview-Of-Medical-Acupuncture

5. Lee, C., Crawford, C., Wallerstedt, D., York, A., Duncan, A., Smith, J., . . . Jonas, W. (2012). The effectiveness of acupuncture research across components of the trauma spectrum response (tsr): A systematic review of reviews. *Systematic Reviews, 1*, 46. doi:10.1186/2046-4053-1-46

6. Kim, Y. D., Heo, I., Shin, B. C., Crawford, C., Kang, H. W., & Lim, J. H. (2013). Acupuncture for post-traumatic stress disorder: A systematic review of randomized controlled trials and prospective clinical trials. *Evidence-Based Complementary and Alternative Medicine*, article 615857. doi:10.1155/2013/615857

7. Craig, G. (n.d.). The Gary Craig Official EFT Training Centers. Retrieved from https://www.emofree.com

8. Church, D., Stapleton, P., Mollon, P., Feinstein, D., Boath, E., Mackay, D., & Sims, R. (2018). Guidelines for the treatment of PTSD using clinical EFT (emotional freedom techniques). *Healthcare, 6*(4), 146. doi:10.3390/healthcare6040146

QUESTION 40

1. PTSD: National Center for PTSD. (n.d.). Cognitive processing therapy for PTSD. Retrieved from https://www.ptsd.va.gov/understand_tx/cognitive_processing.asp

QUESTION 41

1. Seppala, E. (2014, May 8). Connectedness & health: The science of social connection. Retrieved from the Stanford University Center for Compassion and Altruism Research and Education website: http://ccare.stanford.edu/uncategorized/connectedness-health-the-science-of-social-connection-infographic

QUESTION 42

1. NAMI. (n.d.). Retrieved from https://www.nami.org/Find-Support /NAMI-Programs/NAMI-Homefront
2. National Suicide Prevention Lifeline. (n.d.). Retrieved from https:// suicidepreventionlifeline.org

QUESTION 43

1. Linehan, M. M. (1993). *Cognitive-behavioral treatment of borderline personality disorder*. New York, NY: Guilford Press.
2. Linehan, M. M. (2015). *DBT skills training manual* (2nd ed.). New York, NY: Guilford Press.
3. Bateman, A., & Fonagy, P. (2016). *Mentalization-based treatment for personality disorders: A practical guide*. Oxford: Oxford University Press.
4. Bateman, A., & Fonagy, P. (2010). Mentalization-based treatment for borderline personality disorder. *World Psychiatry*, 9(1), 11–15. doi:10.1002/j.2051-5545.2010.tb00255.x
5. Bateman, A., & Fonagy, P. (2013). Mentalization-based treatment. *Psychoanalytic Inquiry*, 33(6), 595–613. doi:10.1080/07351690.2013 .835170
6. Juul, S., Lunn, S., Poulsen, S., Sørensen, P., Salimi, M., Jakobsen, J. C., . . . Simonsen, S. (2019). Short-term versus long-term mentalization-based therapy for outpatients with subthreshold or diagnosed borderline personality disorder: A protocol for a randomized clinical trial. *Trials*, 20(1), 196. doi:10.1186/s13063-019-3306-7
7. Young, J. E., Klosko, J. S., & Weishaar, M. E. (2003). *Schema therapy: A practitioner's guide*. New York, NY: Guilford Press.
8. Kellogg, S. H., & Young, J. E. (2006). Schema therapy for borderline personality disorder. *Journal of Clinical Psychology*, 62(4), 445–458. Retrieved from http://ritayounan.com/wp-content/uploads/2015/03 /kellogyoung-article-sft-for-BPD.pdf
9. Choi-Kain, L. W., Finch, E. F., Masland, S. R., Jenkins, J. A., & Unruh, B. T. (2017). What works in the treatment of borderline personality disorder. *Current Behavioral Neuroscience Reports*, 4(1), 21–30. doi:10.1007/s40473-017-0103-z

QUESTION 44

1. PTSD: National Center for PTSD. (n.d.-a). PTSD treatment basics. Retrieved from https://www.ptsd.va.gov/understand_tx/tx_basics.asp
2. Department of Veterans Affairs, & Department of Defense. (2017). *VA/DOD clinical practice guideline for the management of post-traumatic*

stress disorder and acute stress disorder. Washington, DC: Authors. Retrieved from https://www.healthquality.va.gov/guidelines/MH /ptsd/VADoDPTSDCPGFinal.pdf

3. Beck, A. T., Rush, A. J., Shaw, B. E., & Emery, G. (1987). *Cognitive therapy of depression*. The Guilford clinical psychology and psychopathology series. New York, NY: Guilford Press.

4. Sobel, A. A., Resick, P. A., & Rabalais, A. E. (2009). The effect of cognitive processing therapy on cognitions: Impact statement coding. *Journal of Traumatic Stress, 22*(3), 205–211. doi:10.1002/jts.20408

5. Resick, P. A., Wachen, J. S., Dondanville, K. A., Pruiksma, K. E., Yarvis, J. S., Peterson, A. L., . . . the STRONG STAR Consortium. (2017). Effect of group vs. individual cognitive processing therapy in active-duty military seeking treatment for post-traumatic stress disorder: A randomized clinical trial. *JAMA Psychiatry, 74*(1), 28–36. doi:10.1001/jamapsychiatry.2016.2729

6. PTSD: National Center for PTSD. (n.d.-b) Cognitive processing therapy for PTSD. Retrieved from https://www.ptsd.va.gov/understand_tx /cognitive_processing.asp

7. Alexander, W. (2012). Pharmacotherapy for post-traumatic stress disorder in combat veterans: Focus on antidepressants and atypical antipsychotic agents. *P & T, 37*(1), 32–38. Retrieved from https:// www.ncbi.nlm.nih.gov/pmc/articles/PMC3278188

8. Department of Veterans Affairs, & Department of Defense. (2017). *VA/DOD clinical practice guideline for the management of post-traumatic stress disorder and acute stress disorder*. Washington, DC: Authors. Retrieved from https://www.healthquality.va.gov/guidelines/MH/ptsd /VADoDPTSDCPGFinal.pdf

9. Reisman, M. (2016). PTSD treatment for veterans: What's working, what's new, and what's next. *P & T, 41*(10), 623–634. Retrieved from https://www.ncbi.nlm.nih.gov/pmc/articles/PMC5047000

QUESTION 46

1. Bryant-Davis, T. [drthema]. (2019, May 18). When trauma has shaped you, try not to confuse who you had to become with who you can be [Tweet]. Retrieved from https://twitter.com/drthema/status /1129621494709882881

Index

About the Author

Keith A. Young, LCPC, CCTP, CH, is a licensed counselor, certified clinical trauma professional and certified hypnotherapist with a private practice in Bangor, Maine. He has taught at Husson University and New England College. Young is a member of the American Counseling Association and has been trained in a variety of evidence-based treatments validated for trauma, including eye movement desensitization and reprocessing, trauma-focused cognitive behavioral therapy, and prolonged exposure therapy, as well as dialectical behavior therapy for treatment of borderline personality disorder. He has specialized in the treatment of trauma for more than 18 years.